I2K – Illumaniti C2K – Consciousness in the New Age –

Illuminati Knight Templar Secrets in the 21ˢᵗ Century – The Evolution of Consciousness in a Spiritual World

By George Mentz, Three Initiates, Magus Incognito, Theron Q. Dumont, Swami Panchadasi, Yogi Ramacharaka, Swami Bhakta Vishita

I2K – Illumaniti C2K – Consciousness in the New Age –

Contents

I2K – Illumaniti C2K – Consciousness in the New Age –

I2K – Illumaniti C2K – Consciousness in the New Age –

Awakening of Consciousness – Human Potential

Herein, we are talking about how to awaken from the illusion and develop your powers of perception, and learn to see the world in a smarter way while being more cognitive, and more responsive than 99% of the rest of the world's population. The first question is do you believe in a intelligent life force, an abundant world, or a beneficent spirit of the universe. The spiritually enlightened person might say I don't believe, but I know there is a framework and force, more powerful than gravity that controls the great laws of metaphysics, success and happiness. To begin with, the key really is to learn to look in the mirror and respect & love creation. Herein, we will discuss further ideas to help you tap into the intelligent force of the universe where we can begin to transcend the unseen laws of nature and reach your authentic potential.

We're all evolving in human consciousness. We're all created for a purpose. How can you get closer to your "raison d'etre" or your Reason to Be. And as St. Augustine implied, it's unnecessary to struggle. There's no need for unnecessary suffering. If we were willing to draw closer to the life force of the universe, we can grow and change without needless struggle. In Buddhism, the source of suffering is Trishna which is "clinging or grasping". In the I Ching, the Book of Changes advises students to take action in tandem with the momentum of their life. Therefore, what can we do to hack the brain and go to the next level of speculative and operative metaphysics.

Limited Consciousness

In Matthew, 6:33, it says seek the Kingdom of God first and its righteousness, and everything will be added to you. Therefore, we must decide to accept the power and wisdom and love of the universe into our heart and our mind. The biggest problem most people have is "EP – emotional poverty". We need to rise out of emotional poverty and become emotionally awake and develop emotional power or self-regard and self compassion. So, we may need to seek to identify and destroy mental attachment and ideas that would limit us and our potential and our happiness. Sometimes, we just need to force ourselves to see the good and the beauty and the joy in the moments of each day. To just pause, take a time out to look around, to become aware. To see your surroundings and pick things out that you can enjoy, or admire, or praise, or think of in a positive way. And, visualize and pray for what you know can be in your life, and seek truth internally and externally.

I2K – Illumaniti C2K – Consciousness in the New Age –

Consciousness or C2K.

C2K or "Consciousness in the 21st Century" are the secrets of cultivating a higher intelligence-consciousness where your body, and your mind, and your soul are all operating at a higher level of performance in tandem.

Because a higher consciousness is a Holy Grail of most spiritual seekers. The first secret is trying to seek universal inspiration and tap into the collective consciousness.

We all want our body, mind and your soul to be free of impurities and we go through a process of Catharsis on mental and spiritual level to become a more loving, forgiving and peaceful person.

As we continue to keep our mind effective and free, we are taking care of ourselves by not tainting our body with things that will make us confused or irrational.

If you do all these things then you will be tapped into the collective consciousness in a way we have flow of ideas. It's a different kind of flow. There's a flow state but then there is also a flow mind and I'm talking about the flow mind, the FM. And when you are connected and clear you have a consciousness that brings in ideas and inspiration.

We now discuss the five senses and how they're used. Generally speaking normal consciousness sticks to the five senses; the taste, the feel, the smell, the sound and the vision, and how you see things.

All of that is how you perceive the world and how you view the world is really what your journey is composed of. What your experience is as based on your intake. But if you turn that back and flip it over: if you optimize your body, mind, and soul, then you have an opportunity to enhance and improve the five senses that you have.

The mind operates in the present while utilizing the past. And those two things come together to make the future. So from a standpoint of higher consciousness, it is intriguing to think that the Native Americans and the Shamans of Eurasia really had a greater grasp of the present and the past and what makes the future. They knew how to live in the now and how present-action actually creates who you are and your future.

The Holographic World or Mental Science - Postulates and Concepts

1. Our most important quest must begin within ourselves with an esoteric inner enhancement that connects us to the power, creativity, and wisdom of the universe. The inner transformation must be won before looking to external fixes.

2. Consciousness has evolved instinctively until the 20th Century. Now we have a choice to make intelligent individual mental evolution.

3. There is One Power and that power can be tapped into if we desire to have an efficient mind and conscious harmonious connection with the Spirit of the Universe.

4. The Deeper Mind and Authentic Consciousness have the ability to: Master Imagination, Receive Intelligent Inspiration and Intuition, and even develop types of prescience or psychic powers that allow for a higher order of deductive reasoning, thought and action.

5. The practice of the presence of God is getting ourselves into a consciousness of our oneness and harmony with God or the Universal Life Force.

6. The true teaching of Master was the divine possibility of human potential "Be ye perfect."

7. Practical metaphysics says that you can have anything you earnestly desire as we cannot really desire anything that is not already within us seeking expression.

8. Our potential comes out of an intuitive awareness of our inner potential which is a knowingness with an open heart and mind.

9. We can learn the power of willingness to impress ideas and beliefs upon our subconscious minds and to take action.

10. The key is taking responsibility for our thoughts. Our thoughts occur in mind and are enhanced as a result of our attitudes and feelings.

11. We must work to awaken the mind and allow mindfulness.

12. Robert Frost writes, "First thing I do in the morning is make up my bed, then I make up my mind."

13. Words, attitudes and beliefs are an important part of programming your past, present and future. For by thy words thou shalt be justified, and by thy words thou shalt be condemned. " Matthew 12:36-37

14. To have clarity and mental power, we must remain strong and pure of mind. ** Each day should be analyzed so that you may enhance productivity. Each destructive habit can be analyzed and pruned. Distractive thinking should be set aside. The highest meaning of the past events should be cultivated.. Lessons learned from past experiences should be respected. A healthy respect for the destructive power of certain people, places and things should be honored.

15. How do I want things to be? Who do I want to be? What do I need to be to become the ideal?

16. The first step is to construct a mental prototype, archetypal idea or mental equivalent. If the imagination is practiced, the deeper mind will work 24/7 to assist you in your objectives in conjunction with your impression of the idea on the creative life force.

17. Affirmations have power because they are decreed from a spiritual consciousness. From the work we can speak with confidence, constructiveness and harmony with the universe. The law is set in motion with the word and written word.

18. We must prepare ourselves mentally each day. Each mental seed will bring forth after its kind, feeling and intention.

19. Visualizations have power when imagined with a spiritual intent and feeling. Any desired result projected on the mental picture screen of your inner mind, will become an emblazoned potentiality.

20. Judge Troward emphasizes the power of deep and heart felt feeling when engaging decrees, affirmation, imagination, and visualization. Know with calm

aspiration that all conditions and substance is available for the manifestation of your ideals.

21. Inspiration is created by the WILL and Willingness to receive it. When we are open to Spirit; then, vivifying thoughts, ideas and feelings will flow into us.

22. Meet the Spirit of the Universe 1/2 way with your mind, thinking, ideas and actions.

23. Know with constructive awareness that the beneficent abundant universe will present opportunity and solutions for you to act upon the completion of your objectives.

24. From this day forward, practice mental constructive thinking. Become determined to think and speak in a way that builds your character, beliefs and your reality.

25. When mind is made up, it continues to exercise creative power and sets to work out the purpose of that intention and focus.

26. Spirit and Substance work together: Substance supplies something from which a selection can be made and action can be imparted where the manifestation of our future is an expressing of spirit.

27. Take action upon your ideas and inspiration provided to you to complete your daily tasks and obligations that lead to your purpose and fulfillment.

28. Spirit creates by self contemplation. What you contemplate as the law of your being, becomes your reality.

29. Faith is the substance of things unseen. Faith is Focused Energy. Applied faith is a bit of constructive energy instilled into a belief or an idea or even a healing. All things in balance, an extra bit of faith can stack the energy and potentialities in your favor.

30. If you are determined to utilize your will to make yourself more sick, you can achieve this, but in the same vein, you may use your will and determination to become more healthy, vibrant, enthusiastic, aware, and mindful.

31. A pure harmonious relationship with the universe is what allows for a cosmic metaphysical marriage. This unification can allow anyone to become a master of their destiny.

32. We cultivate the consciousness of oneness with God. To do this, we engage Contemplation or Prayer which is the consciousness of the all-ness of life. Contemplative prayer is a systematic, scientific way of expanding our thoughts and getting in tune with the universal flow of energy. "Be still and know that I am" (Psalms 46:10) and in that stillness, listen.

33. To cultivate an idea, objective or desire into true purpose, we must be receptive and have a WILLINGNESS to achieve it. Our will assists in the molding of the faculty of imagination rightly.

34. The subconscious reasons deductively. Our manifest life is a process of becoming, and we can evolve into new excellence or creativity each day.

35. Consciousness is generator which provides the degree of love, joy, and peace we radiate into ourselves and outward.

36. While there are many ingredients to the recipes of harmony or prayer, gratitude is a key term as it dispels discouragement and allows for a living faith, flow and effective consciousness.

37. Your mental and spiritual consciousness will determine your world view. Your world view will dramatically affect your experience and journey. Thus the totality of your daily thoughts, thinking, actions and omissions IS the Quality of your consciousness.

38. With action and work, it must be in the Here and Now. It must be with focus and contemplativeness. It should not be with anxious thought. If we believe in our purpose and objectives, it will energize our actions and thought.

Each day is an opportunity to take steps in the direction of the desired ideals, , higher consciousness, harmony, and higher order

7 Habits of Those with Higher Consciousness

Habit #1 Metaphysics and Spiritual Economics

The fact remains is that economics has been defined in the United States as a science of scarcely allocated resources, and that is just simply not true. There is unlimited resources, and every time a resource runs low, whether it be here or somewhere else, someone creates a substitute for that thing that is becoming scarce, i.e., that a definition of technology is the creation of new products and services that satisfy needs and demands of humanity.

So here we are at this juncture and what I'm going to say is that You are the totality of your thinking, your actions and your inactions, and that is also your consciousness. You are the totality of your consciousness. Wallace Wattle said, "Every thought or form held in thinking substance causes the creation of the form, but always or at least generally, along the lines of growth an action already established." In general he's saying if you impress your thoughts and your creative visualization and picture the images clearly in your mind, if you cultivate these thoughts and think about it all day long, you develop a consciousness of what you want as having being accomplished, that form will manifest itself either in you or for you. Mr. Neville Goddard has said, "It is only by a change of consciousness, by actually changing your concept of yourself that you can build more stately mansions, the manifestations of higher and higher concepts." Most all of these authors, whether it be Napoleon Hill in the 1920s, Wallace Wattles in 1910, Charles Haanel in 1910; all of these major writers are saying the same thing, that you must have a burning desire to change, a burning desire to do something, and what that means is a purpose, where you realize what you want to do and you'd be willing to do anything you can to achieve it.

Habit #2 Mental Ownership - Pre-Assumption or Presuming

And here we come upon the great concept of presumption or the concept of having something in your mind or in your consciousness. Presumption is a wonderful thing because if you presume that you're going to have something and you keep doing that day in and day out and you keep taking action to achieve that presumption day in and day out, then it becomes your goal, your primary purpose, where you'll begin to create the snowball effect of moving the momentum of your mind and your energy towards a particular result. In some cases, you're going to have to let go of your old self altogether and some spiritually minded people would say that you have to let your old self die out and the new person that you want to be to be reborn or be reinvented. And here's the thing: if you want to be something and you're going to be it, you're going to start acting like it or faking it till you make it. If you want to be a Wall Street investment banker, then you're going to have to start playing the part of a Wall Street investment banker. You're going to have to know and understand the rules and the laws and the investment regulations related to being an investment banker. You have to become that person. You would associate with people who are in the business. You have to act the part, and that's what separates mere thinking from being. So the real question of the day is you can learn about the metaphysics, you can do the exercises, you can do the affirmations, but at some point you have to be and act the part, and also you have to know and feel in your heart and in your mind that the results you want belong to you. And the other urgent issue is that you need to understand the essence of what you want. Why do you want something, and if you achieve it, how are you going to use that achievement? How are you going to take advantage of the achievement? How are you going to enjoy the achievement?

Habit #3 Affirmations and Contemplation – Change your Vibe

As stated in Elizabeth Towne's famous books, "The treatment for success is the same as for health; repeated affirmations, present tense, positive mood. I AM what I desire to manifest." What does this all mean? Here is an example of one of the first complete affirmations for health written over one hundred years ago by Wallace Wattles. Read this carefully a few time, and you will come to know the conscious power of healing of divine mind.

With the development of our imagination, we learn to picture our goals and dreams in our mind. We further discover how to affirm and cultivate a feeling that "All is right with my World" Begin at home and learn to build relationships with complements, praise and support. Prayer and visualization and feeling are linked on a spiritual and universal level. An affirmation or prayer should be utilized in a way that invokes feeling and energy to the core of your spirit. This can be called cognitive cellular transformation CCT. Using prayer, visualization and affirmations must be optimized so that your consciousness is lifted up. If you must hit your knees or gently tap your chest while praying, these techniques can help infuse your spirit with a higher energy and higher connection with the spiritual source of all. Seeing the results of your visualization or affirmation in your mind's eye is part of the visualization process. Feeling what you see in your mind's eye is yet another step.

Quotes:
- Now faith is the assurance of things hoped for, the conviction of things not seen. For by it the people of old received their commendation. By faith we understand that the universe was created by the word of God, so that what is seen was not made out of things that are visible. Hebrews 11:1-3
- Jesus answered him, "Truly, truly, I say to you, unless one is born again he cannot see the kingdom of God." John 3:3
- "I learned this, at least, by my experiment: that if one advances confidently in the direction of his dreams, and endeavors to live the life which he has imagined, he will meet with a success unexpected in common hours." — Henry David Thoreau, Walden: Or, Life in the Woods

A Classic Abundant Health Exercise and Meditation

Take a time when you can have from twenty minutes to half an hour secure from interruption, and proceed first to make yourself physically comfortable. Lie at ease in a chair, or on a couch, or in bed; it is best to lie flat on your back. If you have no other time, take the exercise on going to bed at night and before rising in the morning.

First let your attention travel over your body from the crown of your head to the soles of your feet, relaxing every muscle as you go. Relax completely. And next, get physical and other ills off your mind. Let the attention pass down the spinal cord and out over the nerves to the extremities, and as you do so think: "My nerves are in perfect order all over my body. They obey my will, and I have great nerve force." Next bring your attention to the lungs and think: "I am breathing deeply and quietly, and the air goes into every cell of my lungs, which are in perfect condition. My blood is purified and made clean." Next, to the heart: "My heart is beating strongly and steadily, and my circulation is perfect, even to the extremities."

Next, to the digestive system: "My stomach and intestines perform their work perfectly. My food is digested and assimilated and my body rebuilt and nourished. My liver, kidneys, and bladder each perform their several functions without pain or strain; I am perfectly well. My body is resting, my mind is quiet, and my soul is at peace."

Next: "I have no anxiety about financial or other matters. God, who is within me, is also in all things I want, impelling them toward me; all that I want is already given to me. I have no anxiety about my health, for I am perfectly well. I have no worry or fear whatever. "I rise above all temptation to moral evil. I cast out all greed, selfishness, and narrow personal ambition; I do not hold envy, malice, or enmity toward any living soul. I will follow no course of action which is not in accord 'with my highest ideals. I am right and I will do right.'"

Viewpoint

All is right with the world. It is perfect and advancing to completion. I will contemplate the facts of social, political, and industrial life only from this high viewpoint. Behold, it is all very good. I will see all human beings, all my acquaintances, friends, neighbors, and the members of my own household in the same way. They are all good. Nothing is wrong with the Universe; nothing can be wrong but my own personal attitude, and henceforth I keep that right. My whole trust is in God.

Consecration

I will obey my soul and be true to that within me that is highest. I will search within for the pure idea of right in all things, and when I find it I will express it in my outward life. I will abandon everything I have outgrown for the best I can think. I will have the highest thoughts concerning all my relationships, and my manner and action shall express these thoughts. I surrender my body to be ruled by my mind; I yield my mind to the dominion of my soul, and I give my soul to the guidance of God.

Identification and Reconciliation

There is but one substance and source, and of that I am made and with it I am one. It is my Father; I proceeded forth and came from it. My Father and I are one, and my Father is greater than I, and I do His will. I surrender myself to conscious unity with Pure Spirit; there is but one and that one is everywhere. I am one with the Eternal Consciousness.

Idealization

Form a mental picture of yourself as you want to be, and at the greatest height your imagination can picture. Dwell upon this for some little time, holding the thought: "This is what I really am; it is a picture of my own perfection and advancing to completion. I will contemplate the facts of social, political, and industrial life only from this high viewpoint. Behold, it is all very good. I will see all human beings, all my acquaintances, friends, neighbors, and the members of my own household in the same way. They are all good. Nothing is wrong with the Universe, nothing can he wrong but my own personal attitude, and henceforth I keep that right. My whole trust is in God.

Realization

I appropriate to myself the power to become what I want to be, and to do what I want to do. I exercise creative energy; all the power there is, is mine. I will arise and go forth with power and perfect confidence; I will do mighty works in the strength of the Lord, my God. I will trust and not fear, for God is with me. [i]

• Remember that simple pains and discomforts are sometimes signals to take action to better your physical health; however, many pains are the body at work healing and regenerating itself on a cellular and molecular level.

• As a note, you may be able to work this positive person in your MIND for other people.

Other Affirmations

Prosperity

I am the essence of success. The universe is full of creation and expands every day. New opportunities and new ideas flow to me. I open my heart to that power and participate in the divine ideas that come to me every minute of the day. I allow peace and prosperity in my heart, mind, and soul. I know that I am blessed, and I am thankful for the gift of creation and life expression.

Health

My body is a temple of creation; every organ in my body is nourished and revitalized each day. In time, my whole physical being is regenerated cell by cell. My mental ideal of myself is perfect. Because I am an offspring of perfect creation, I am made uniquely wonderful through this authority. My body is a vessel of my spirit and soul, which allows me to exist and create in this world. I respect my body and accept the power and opportunity of life, living and wholeness.

Attitude

My inner spiritual condition allows me to have a high viewpoint of the world. I see the world as a place of kindness, and I become open to receiving the blessings of goodness from others. I see the best in others and myself. I am worthy of success and a wonderful life.

Love

I do all I can to maintain a consciousness of love in my mind. I forgive all those who have passed through my life. I want the best for everyone and hope that all can live in harmony, peace, love, and abundance. I meditate on the words of compassion, understanding, peace, humility, kindness, generosity, and selflessness.

Gratitude

I am grateful to all those who have come before me. I am thankful to the supreme creative power for life, peace, health, and the ability to love. Gratitude and a thankful heart keep me connected to power. Gratitude allows me to have faith and the knowledge that I can exist in a higher order of being.

Success

I am successful. I am worthy of prosperity, abundance, health, and happiness. Each day my life becomes better and better.

Habit #4 - Tune-Up the System – Getting Clear with Power

Before you start focusing on your creative abilities and focusing on manifesting something new and concentrating on changing so much, sometimes you need to go through and take a hard look at your life, take a look at the last three, five and 10 years, and make an analysis of the successes and failures over this period. Begin an inventory of these years and find out the things that have been good for you and find out your actions and thinking that has been not constructive for you, and then what you need to do is learn to prune the tree.

Learn to let go of the old things that haven't been useful and constructive for you, and then allow the things that have been good about you to stay and begin to cultivate these constructive things. This will clear the slate and all you to begin anew. Then, ultimately you'll have more room in your heart and your mind to allow this new you, this new thinking or this fresh consciousness into your heart.

Now you may need to talk to a spiritual advisor or a life coach or a therapist or somebody like that about these things, you can talk them through so that you can let go and get some closure and some catharsis on these old issues, and that's fine. But once you let go of all that junk, trim away all of that mental garbage, you have created some spiritual space, some empty space in your mental garden to allow new things to flourish.

And here's the thing: the reason you want to do that is you don't want to have a mentality that is a "house divided". If you're dragging along a whole bunch of old baggage of negative thinking or resentments or anger or ego related issues or hurt, there's got to be a way out of this. You've got to make a conscious decision to allow yourself to be helped, to allow your soul to let go of any negative past, because if you don't let go of all of the downbeat stuff, you're going to have all that on your mind and it's going to be one voice arguing with your new voice, and you don't want a house divided.

You want to be able to let go of that stuff so you can start fresh and get that reinvention that I talked about earlier. And if you have done the work and you've cleared away all the stuff that you don't want anymore in your life, there's going to be less distraction going forward, and you'll be more focused and you'll have more concentration and more controlled imagination, and these are the things that are ultimately going to help you propel yourself rapidly towards your new goals and objectives. Now ultimately, if you go through this catharsis, then you've changed your view, you've changed your feelings, you've changed your imagination, and then guess what, you'll change your behavior and miraculously, you'll change your outcomes.

Habit #5 - CLAIMING IT - Having IT in MIND

Those with a Higher Consciousness use the imagination to formulate the future. They use the secret of cultivating the feeling of having something already. So, to activate the power of presumption, all that we need to learn is to presuppose new destinies or assume success, but we also need to "mentally experience" that success. So thus, we have to change our essential concepts of ourselves and we have to persist in that desire of change until it is fact. We need to "Be that Ideal". We need to "feel the ideal outcome". We have to sustain the attitude that we're open and receptive to the ideal. When I say ideal, I mean the ideal situation, the ideal result, the ideal outcome. So we need to surrender our intention to the new self, to the new essence mentally, and capture the new ideal in-our-mind so that it becomes our dominant thought pattern and mental matrix.

We want a richer and fuller life. And ultimately our destiny is a result of our consciousness in the now, our consciousness *in the moment*. And most of the famous writers in prosperity and metaphysics will say that you have to form a mental image in your mind, on the picture screen in your mind of what you desire or what you want to be, and then you need to learn to concentrate your attention upon this. And great teachers will say that before going to bed and when you wake up in the morning, you must gently think about this new mental picture of yourself, of how you want to be or what you want to achieve or the things you want to have. Think and Feel as though you have it already in your heart and your mind. Cultivate that consciousness of having. And, when you nurture that consciousness of having the best, you're thinking from the position of owning it already as if you were already there in fact. Then ultimately your dominant emotions and mind-set will be fuel for your creation of new forms and creation of new fortunes. And your determined imagination will help fill this vacuum.

For all of us, there comes a point in time when we make a conscious decision that we're not going to put up with the same old negative thinking, the same old scarcity thinking, the same old complaining. Extreme realism is what I would call it, where you're just so realistic that you are determined to be right about what's wrong. There comes a point when all of us wake up one morning and say, "We've got to let go of this". It is holding us back. So as soon as you make a conscious decision to control your thoughts and control your thinking and direct it towards constructive and productive ideals, then you'll be able to energize what you want to manifest in your life. You'll be able to give attention to the things that support your growth. And, you will be able to concentrate on your ideals and cultivate thanks for all the good and the lessons of the past. Then, you can begin to prune the old stuff "out of your life" and allow your imagination to expand to new levels.

And with this new thinking, this new positivism, this new constructive imagination, your dominant self-concept IS *who you are*. This Dominant Mindset is what you will be. And you will have it, you'll use it, you'll feel it and you will be it. Accordingly, your consciousness and your positive feelings regarding your becoming is what will generate your new oncoming reality. To do these things, you will have to sustain a receptiveness in the now, which will avail a new flow of creativity. As I said earlier, sometimes people don't even know what their purpose is supposed to be. Sometimes they don't even know what their burning desire is supposed to be. So when you clear away the mental rubbish and you become receptive, then you avail yourself to this flow of creativity and ideas. And this manifestation of your ideas that are coming from this divine and spiritual flow, that will be your creation. That is your creative ability & where you find desire and purpose.

To put it another way, your creativity is believing in the ideas that you have as presented in a form that already exists. And your assumptions and your awareness or your presumptions and your receptiveness will allow for these preexisting mental forms to manifest themselves. And as I have intimated, your spiritual condition affects your perception and your worldview affects your experience & Raison d'être or "reason to be" which is your true Purpose. Your ongoing conditioning is your power to manifest.

Habit #6 - Acceptance and Gratitude – Mental Prosperity

First of all, acceptance is neither bad nor good; it's a little of both. In a sense, when you accept something you're not just accepting what is wrong. You may be accepting what is well and good. So acceptance is really more of just surrender to what is. It's also being detached in a way that you're wearing life as a loose garment, and this detachment, just like Meister Eckhart said hundreds of years ago, allows you to be free and connected to the spirit of the universe or The Forces of GOD. And once you accept *what is* and realize that most distractions are merely material and external, you will see that the only true dominion and control that you must have is your internal consciousness, thinking, vibration and character. And this positive acceptance can allow you to work on what is internal, the esoteric work, the inner growth, the building of yourself from the inside out, and that is the way that you change your thinking and change the way you see things and change your perception.

Let us look at it this way: if you change the way you feel about yourself, if you change your self-regard, you will change the way you see life and how you experience everything. And this is why a thankful heart or gratitude is so important for all of us. They say that gratitude is probably the one sheer antidote to discouragement. Gratitude is the one power that if you exercise it everyday in your life and you remain thankful in your heart for the ability to walk, talk, see, hear, think, create and all good things things, that you just truly feel the basics of gratitude, this positions your mind into a state of thankfulness and connectedness to the creative power of the universe. It also breaks up the old preconceptions that are blocking you from that divine spiritual connection to the world and the universe such as: greed, pride, lust, anger, gluttony, envy, sloth – all of these things, resentment, jealousy, anger, and on and on it goes. If you develop a sense of gratitude, it will shatter negative mental concepts and allow the sunlight of the spirit to continue to shine upon you.

Being Excellent

Many great writers will talk about increase or value or giving without expectation, and all of these things are key virtues in the expansion and improvement of your life.

What these authors mean by value and <u>increase</u> is that if you provide excellence to other people then you will be known as excellent and a person in increases the life of others. If you give someone quality service with that extra little something, go the extra mile, you will be remembered well by all people. And these acts, one-by-one, of excellence and increase in value conveying the impression to other people that you have the ability to provide advice, services products with skill. diligence and enthusiasm, all of this adds up, and you will become rich, and you will become great, and you will become excellent as a result of this type of behavior.

Habit #7 Creative Visualization & Action

Napoleon Hill, Charles Haanel, and Wallace Wattles all said one thing very strongly, and they said the more clear and definite that you make the picture of our purpose/objective in your mind, the more clear that you make your goal, the more vividly you can see it, the more you know what it looks like and what it feels like to have it, the better your chances are that that ideal or that thing will manifest itself in your life. And in the end, you've got to be able to see your desire and purpose vividly, you've got to be able to experience it in mind, you've got to be grateful on the inside, in your heart, and you've got to cultivate a consciousness of having it, and cultivate a faith that it will be yours.

If you look at any Olympic athlete or professional athlete, whether it be basketball, football, track, or whatever it might be, all of these people are practicing everyday, but they're also conditioning themselves mentally everyday, and seeing themselves doing things everyday in an excellent way. Whether it's putting a football in the end-zone or putting a basketball through the net for a three pointer, or running a marathon in a certain amount of time, these exceptional achievers strive to condition themselves mentally, and that's why seeing yourself doing something is key to a lot of this and also a driver to ACTION. If you already have an idea that the wish can be fulfilled, then you already know that the goal can be accomplished.

As Prof. Wattles, said over a hundred years ago," In order to get rich, you do not need a sweet hour of prayer; you need to pray without ceasing, and by prayer I mean holding steadily to your vision with the purpose to cause it's creation into solid form and the faith that you are doing so." And remember, the best thing you can do for yourself, for your family and for society and humanity is to make the best of yourself and to exercise your talents to their highest ability, because in the end that is what will allow you to give the most and help the most people.

The 12 Characteristics of Magical and Prosperous People

1. **A purpose driven personality** with a desire to express themselves in the most constructive ways.
2. **A worldview and consciousness of possibility,** prosperity and harmlessness
3. People who are beyond competitive and very creative. Visionaries who strive to see and feel the reality of their dreams.
4. **Gratitude minded** – people with a thankful heart and sincere belief in the goodness of the universe.
5. **Boldness, action oriented**, willing to take calculated risks, and Authentic.
6. Self Regard – people who believe that they are worthy of a rich and full life and are willing to work to receive it.
7. **At-Ease – Harmonious mind and thinking**. People willing to cultivate peace of mind and balance in body, mind and spirit.
8. **Love of Fellowship** – willing to help others with time and talent.
9. **Receptivity** - Global & Non-judgmental openness to others' ideas and creativity. Open to inspiration.
10. **A Unique Spirit** – Individualization of soul and spirit. Allowing yourself to become who you are meant to be.
11. **Desire to serve humanity** be being your best. A passion to contribute as an individual to the greater good.
12. **Spiritual Awakenings** - People who have become Spiritually Awake to a higher order of being and work to maintain such a level of thinking, acting and being.

The Power of Consciousness in the Now - Presumption Decoded

Being Contemplative in Action – Getting Into NOW

If you have ever thought deeply about the magical power of the present moment, you may wonder if you have the capability of this type of superior focus and mindfulness. After reviewing all of the major religions on the philosophy on the power of PRESENCE, I have discovded many specific keys to success in being in the moment. To begin with, the theme of the Power of Awareness is to quiet the mind, to calm the self-talk, to learn to control your thoughts while directing your thinking so that you may be present in the moment, to be alive and conscious "right now".

This is not necessarily a Eastern or Western concept, however there are many esoteric & Christian underpinnings herein that are addressed. Firstly, it is advised that we intently listen to our self-talk deep within our mind and then try to truly see and listen to that inner-voice as an observer. Getting to know your ego voice as compared to your authentic spiritual voice of your heart is also a major exercise of this topic.

The easiest example of directing your awareness to the now is to direct your controlled attentiveness to your body, to your breathing, to what you see, what you hear, what you're eating or what you're tasting or who you're with. Whether it's focusing on the aliveness of your child or actually seeing or sensing parts of your own body, you can go deeper into your awareness. Here's an example: Try to actually feel your extremities, actually noticing the feelings in your fingers or feelings in your toes at any given moment. Or, what emotions are going on in your mind or even in your stomach.

If you're like the average person, your mind could be harping on 50 different things at once, like a TV on 50 different channels constantly running, and the real key is to pick a channel and focus on a single concept, one thing at a time, one moment at a time, one day at a time, one instance at a time. Further, we can concentrate on one thing at a time, or we can just be aware to the moment and allow our mind to do what is best for us. As an example, the famous movie The Last Samurai with Tom Cruise, they were talking about no mind. To NOT overthink everything is what a teacher would mean by no mind, not overthinking every single move or every single tactic. And just like driving, the first time you drive the car or stick shift, there's many things that you're learning how to do that sooner or later becomes something embedded in your subconscious or in your machinery, and you automatically can get in a car and know exactly what you need to do. So the key really is to be able to program the way you live to think and live in a way that doesn't require you to overthink everything. This process allows you to exist in your real-time state of aliveness.

After rereading books on mysticism and self empowerment, many of us have an awakening of consciousness, a spiritual awakening of sorts, and don't even know how it happened or what had happened and years later we figure out that as a byproduct of reading what other mystics had taught about these types of transformations, we become better people.

However, there are many of us out here in the world who have already had this similar type of awakening, this aliveness, this consciousness, and if you are one of us, you know it deeply. If you're on an enlightened path, you will inherently know it because you can walk in a room with 100 people in it, and you can look around and you actually see people and you're actually alive and you actually know what is happening. And if you're living in this awake-ness, you will have the ability to control what's going on in your mind and your thoughts, and you will have the ability to choose and decide the type of thinking that you will have all day long, and in the end the type of thinking that you have all day long, the type of actions you do all day long, the person who you are, who you become all day long. Then that's who and what you REALLY are. That is what you will become.

So in total, if you're able to control your thinking and you're able to control who you are and the totality of your actions and inactions; then, you're entirely able to control your destiny and you're able to control what you become.

In books such as the Power of Now, Teachers such as Eckhart Tolle spend a lot of time talking about "no mind" and pain body. And I'm just going to explain it to you right now. Pain body is basically Eckhart Tolle's way of saying that if you're one of these people that's sitting around each day thinking negative thoughts and destructive thoughts and trying to be the victim and trying to identify with all this negative stuff and complaining all the time while also trying to blame everyone except yourself or your situation, That is the pain body. You can learn about ego related negativism in church, from a life coach, or in various spiritual venues. However, Tolle's book s was the most popular manuscript to codify the concepts.

And what I'm saying is that if you have this ego that's wrapped up in this identity and it's trying to protect itself, it's not going to want to take a look in the mirror. Your ego is not going to want to change. It's not going to want to accept responsibility for your life and the way you are and what's become of you. So if you can break free of that ego bondage and find your spiritual self, your true inner self, who you really are and get in touch with that and get in touch with the spirituality within, then all the sudden this unlimited flow and this unlimited potentiality becomes available to you, and that's where this aliveness comes from. And, that's what the Christians talk about being *contemplative in action* and also Christians also talk about the Holy Spirit, which is basically that connectedness and that non-separateness, that *spiritual, god-unity* that every religion around the world talks about.

Once you enter this aliveness and this newfound awakening and this consciousness, you'll have no need to defend yourself. You'll have no desire to overreact to things. You'll have this true power within. And also you'll have this now consciousness, which determines how you effectively manifest things. Let's put it this way: if you're able to develop a new consciousness of aliveness, a higher consciousness of success, a greater consciousness of action and doing things, this ***"in the moment"*** consciousness is what will transmute ideas into success and transform possibility into taking mental form, bring ideas into material tangible form on this plane.

In many other religions or spiritual movements, you'll hear the word 'acceptance' and being able to accept what is. It is what it is or accept the now or accept the good and accept the bad and let go of it. Because this is in essence what will free you from present pain in the mind that's saying that you should be in pain.

Furthermore, this idea of knowingness is what you really want. You want to know and believe that you could control your destiny, and if you don't know and you don't believe, then you might be sitting around wishing for something to happen or hoping for something to happen, and it can keep you stuck in the past, or the future. And it can keep you from realizing your dreams if your ego and your "self" is so identified with things that are wrong with the world. If you can change your train of thoughts and change how you think, you'll be able to have your mind focus on what is right with the world and look at what is good and what is beautiful. And if you start focusing on all the good and the beautiful and the rightness and the righteousness of the world and its impersonal nature, you'll be able to attract more of that.

The Power of Esoteric Spirituality and Metaphysics

In essence, developing metaphysical power is an inside job. This is an esoteric science, this power of now. So being able to control what goes on the inside is esoteric and it's what spiritual and religious and philosophical leaders have been talking about since Pythagoras, Socrates, Plato, Confucius, Buddha, Aristotle and all the rest. They've been talking about these metaphysical concepts since the beginning of civilization. If you can master yourself, you'll be able to master your destiny and have a great effect upon those around you and do a great service for humanity.

What is great about The Power of Now or being in the moment with your consciousness, it allows you to compartmentalize the day, which keeps you from being paralyzed by any situations and you're able to free the mind of attachments. And if you can free the mind of too much junk that's floating around in it, you're able to focus and concentrate and direct your energies into the areas that will most improve your life from the inside out.

Additionally, attention is energy, so you need to remember what you focus on expands in your life. You need to choose and decide what to energize with your attention in any given moment. So like I said before, the pain body is this negative energy of the ego mind, and if you're able to get your attention away from that and give your attention to things that are constructive and positive and reinvigorating, then that's what you want to do because if you give your attention to the pain body, guess what? That's fuel that will keep pain flowing and going. Those who teach about the power of the PRESENT also write a lot about how your conscious mind and your subconscious mind coexist, or rather, how to transcend your ego elf to begin to listen to your spiritual voice.

I2K – Illumaniti C2K – Consciousness in the New Age –

It's like this, all of us really need to tap into that spiritual self, which is basically the best friend that you had growing-up when you were child. Now you know that there's an old adage that says that some children have their little best friend, their *imaginary* friend, which is really their spiritual higher-self that they are embracing and befriending and their imagination allows them to love that part of themselves without limitation. However, a lot of children lose that magical relationship at a very early age. We know this story. We've seen it time and time again, so we know that this spiritual self, this best friend, that's the relationship that we need to cultivate. The relationship with our spiritual self and our relationship with the spirit of the universe should come first for us to maximize our peace and prosperity.

So anyway, some of these famous authors of days gone by have said that when you have a grateful mind and a thankful heart, it is a lot easier to have a living faith. Thus a mind of joy cannot support pain body or negative thinking. So the best thing that we can all do for ourselves to change our worldview is to change how we think and change our state of gratitude. As the famous philosopher Magus Incognito once said, each person's worldview is based on their spiritual condition.

So the word 'alchemy' really is transmuting one substance into another substance, and here if you could change your lower self into your higher self, if you could transcend from your ego into your spiritual essence, that is the real key to these teachings. Transmutation is achieved by the conscious contact with the spirit of the universe. Transmutation is achieved through the consciousness of love, the consciousness of wisdom, the consciousness of gratitude and joy.

The other issue in the power of the moment is how many of us are addicted to the adrenaline of anger or self-righteousness or justified anger and blame, and unfortunately that's why social justice has become such a trendy thing is because it can get you so riled up about blaming somebody for something that happened a long time ago when in essence if we focused all that very same time and energy for inner social justice, the whole world would probably change for the better.

And the other thing of this is that if we surround ourselves with sick people, angry people, people who are not alive, people who are realists, who think the world is bad, that type of attitude is contagious, and unfortunately as spiritual seekers, we want to be close to those who want a spiritual life.

And if we can draw close to those who have the same general desire of wholeness and aliveness and health, then we will all become healthier much quicker, and this of course is why self-help groups and fellowships of sorts have become so popular over the last 30, 40, 50 years.

And really the theme of NOW reminds of flow, reminds me of detachment. Meister Eckhart talked a lot about detachment. And we're talking about non-resistance, and there's just so many times in our lives where you can just let go and thrive. Accordingly, some of the biggest miracles in our lives happen when we're not fighting something, we have our mouths shut and we just allow things to pass us by. We have to know when to FLOW and when to pick our battles and know when to stand up for ourselves, but in general, 99% of the time we're going to be okay if we can just stay calm in the moment and allow people to just be.

Once you have developed this aliveness and this consciousness, this higher order in your life, you know what it tastes like and you're going to want more of it, and you're going to do the things that you can do to stay in tune and embrace and own it because it feels so good to be alive and to be clear and if we keep our minds somewhat clear and we do the things we need to do each day or each week to maintain like to spirit, that clarity and that peace of mind will be available and afforded to us.

In the end, this is about surrender. It's about "surrender to win". If you let go of the things that are hurting you, you're able to move forward and not have to drag a lot of dead weight along with you anymore. And then you'll learn to act with purpose and clarity and focus because you're not carrying all this useless baggage. And, then you'll learn to do all you can in the now. And this surrender really unveils your spiritual power.

So in essence, a lot of religions and movements, spiritual groups talk about this key to power, being free and clearing the mind. When you're able to master yourself, you're able to let go of all the junk in the past, you're able to create this space inside of you and allow some joy and greatness to come into your life for the first time.

I2K – Illumaniti C2K – Consciousness in the New Age –

Some people refer to it as a spiritual vacuum, and this vacuum, once you clear stuff out, it creates space in a vacuum and something has to fill it. And if you're in the power of now and you have this consciousness of good and you believe and you know that the world will take care of you in spite of everything that's going on, then good things will come to you. Good people, good ideas, good opportunities, good health and so forth will all be available to you.

So in summary, what is The Power of Now to me and what can it be to you? It's developing this relaxed and free awareness of the now, of the moment and in that relaxed free awareness you become receptive and awake to the good and the beautiful things in the world such as gratitude, health, aliveness, optimism, knowingness, and you're "I am-ness" or "spiritual and divine energy/presence" is made available to you. And what is the "I am"? The "I am" is your presence, is your spiritual self that is talked about in the old wisdom literature. And you become conscious of the now field of energy, which you will master and learn to control what is in that energy, that totality of it, and that becomes who you are.

And if you're anything like me or other people, when you wake up one morning, after having been engaging gratitude in your daily life and you begun clearing the baggage out of your past and using these methods and these steps of developing clarity, you begin letting go of all of the mental rubbish or clutter that has weighed you down. Then, you will find that you want to practice gratitude on a daily basis, you start to practice peace of mind on a daily basis and cultivating a thankful heart and a thankful mind on a daily basis. And behold, one morning sometime soon you're going to REALLY wake up and you're going to wake up on the RIGHT side of the bed, and you're going to KNOW it. And then a few days later, if you keep practicing this consciousness of love and consciousness of God and consciousness of good, you might wake up again like that, and then all of the sudden you'll continue to wake up on the right side of the bed and you'll look forward to the days and you'll be alive and want to do things each day for yourself and other people and participate in life. And all of that aliveness and that now-ness and that spiritual awakeness is what dissipates this pain body and this negative thinking.

So in conclusion, you and a lot of other people, once you become awake, you're going to be so thrilled and energized by it that you're going to be changed, you're going to

I2K – Illumaniti C2K – Consciousness in the New Age –

want to repudiate generalized negative thinking, and if you hear other people talking about negative thinking and pessimistic stuff and wasteful stuff, you're not going to want to be around them.

What I'm saying, if you hear your own voice in your mind and you're observing your mind complaining and trying to justify and blame and seek all this stuff, you're going to tell it to stop. You're going to want to wake up alive and on the right side of the bed and in tune with the infinite and connected to the world, and you're going to want to wake up and see the beauty of life, and regardless of what bad things happen.

And if you're anything like me or most people in general, we have all had some big challenges….. I've gone through tragedies like Hurricane Katrina. I've lost loved ones, including my father. I've lost businesses, had people steal lots from me, and I've had burdens just like everyone else. I've had losses and defeats and pain and real catastrophic events in my life, but when you achieve this aliveness and this consciousness of now, you know that you can move on and you can prevail and even go to greater heights regardless of what happens because you truly have yourself and you have your unity, your empowerment, and your earnest connection to the Spirit of the Universe.

Power of Past and Present

Historically, there are nuggets of truth that many do not know about the power of now. And, through my studies of ancient shamanism in different parts of Asia and Northern Europe, the ancient peoples really did believe that the now is manifested here both in logic and language. And, these Northern tribes believed in only a past and a non-past, and there's no future until you have acted. So, in essence what that means is that "the now creates the future", or the now is the future as a byproduct of the past and present action. So thus, every moment of thought and action becomes the future, the present, and the past which guides and determines a set of pre-destinies or outcomes with variables that may be enhanced by the mind, body, and spirit.

Spiritual Filling and Re-Charging

There is a field of potentiality in the spiritual vacuum, but mind must be organized and cleansed to have that force and pressure to be effectively applied.

Thus, when we want to create a new opportunity or new destiny, we need to realize that we need to purge ourselves in one of 2ways: either that or forcefully fill ourselves with some new information or new good or new ideas to push out the old, or we need to empty and clear our mind and heart and then allow new ideas and good to enter. And, must realize that IN nothing IS something. What that means is nothing is a blank page of your day or your life, and in that vacuum of nothingness it acts like a magnet that is supercharged by intent. So, a blank piece of paper, for instance, in your mind, the picture screen of your mind can be charged with your intent. And, that can become something in the supernatural world of your mind. Furthermore, it is your consciousness or your I-am-ness, or your "is-ness" that creates your consciousness. But, it's also the co-creator and manifestor of your experience and your journey. So basically, your consciousness, or your is-ness, or your mindfulness creates and manifests your experience. So, your worldview or your mental view of the world creates your journey.

Consciousness

What is consciousness? Many refer to the subconscious and the conscious mind as separated into two things. And the consciousness at it's foundation is composed of the 5 senses of: taste, feel, smell, and sound and vision. Those are the main five senses, and consciousness is generally operative on the levels of mind and memory. So, we are either working with what's going on in the present or you are drawing from your memory or a combination of both. And then there is how to train and use the consciousness with general practices and skills of the day.

There is consciousness beyond the traditional senses which can be developed. Just think about what you may be conscious of on a daily basis such as your dreams, intuition, memory, mindfulness, prayer, daydreaming states, meditation, gut feelings, clairaudience, awareness, your sensations and various emotions of wisdom, awe, courage, love.

Two of the higher levels of consciousness and human development are: imagination and intuition. These two are available to all, but few know how to maximize these two aspects of self development, mind control, and consciousness. And the next level of consciousness which I refer to as C2K involves the use of imagination coupled with intuition, and developing those two parts of the mind to act with the power of synthesis of the totality of information. Other areas of training and development of consciousness are symbolism, metaphors, allegories, and parables. These tools and practices help us remember things, or act on information, and learn lessons, of course because we can play the tape back in our heads and respond to our perceptions according to our knowledge.

Prescience and Intuition

This section is about how to develop your intuition or our inspiration. First of all, what's the difference between inspiration and intuition? Well, let's say you start your morning with some meditation. You sit down and you read some meditative books. And, you ponder them and you muse over those ideas that you've read, that information that you've read. And, as you sit peacefully with your quiet mind, while ideas begin to flow to you about what you should do with your day, or some other concern in relation to the reading that you've had.

And, from those ideas you've received some inspiration which technically is a type of intuition. And, this information has come to you, and you need to decide how to act upon it. And, the best way to decide upon any intuition or any inspiration that you've received, an idea from the universe is to filter it through some simple ethical and virtuous principles such as: lovingness, and kindness, and is it pure and good for your mind, is it harmless to other people, is it good for you and other people, is it unselfish and is it loving. Those are just some basic principles that you should use.

Furthermore, the ideas should be backed by some facts so that the idea is a calculated risk but probable success. Thus, if the facts back up your idea, if you act upon the idea with action, belief, intent, planning, and hard work, the probability of success is good.

Examples seeking Prescience and Inspiration Consciousness.

1) One, you might want to go through a guided meditation or guided fantasy of sorts. You can imagine yourself going to a beautiful castle in the mountains, and you arrive there, and you walk into the hall of a beautiful castle room, and you see someone at the throne there, and low and behold, it's you. It's you, but it's the glorified, the wonderful you who's the king or queen of the castle. And, you go and speak directly to that person. You sit down next to them or in front of them or stand in front of them, and you ask questions. And, once you ask a question in your mind's eye, you wait for the answer and see what comes.

   The magic of this mindful practice is that for many people another genuine tone of voice will RESPOND. It's an authentic voice different from yours, and it will give answers to your questions. Like should I take this job, or should I invest in this certain venture, should I be better friends with a certain person, or take the relationship to another level. These are just some basic examples. Or, should I move to a different place, or foreign land, etc.. The goal here is to make friends with your Higher Self and learn to seek the wisdom to the deeper and authentic self which knows your truth and the best answers for you.

2) The second practice or exercise is you go to the same castle in your mind where you go to a special room with a door. Then, you ask a question to yourself before you go to the door, and when the door opens, after you've asked the question, there's either going to be a yes or no in your mind when the door opens.

3) The third way might be to use a card or a rune or some type of decision piece, and you ask a question and you pick the card or the rune or the decision piece, and it can give you an answer, a yes or a no, or maybe, or something descriptive. There're various different types of decision type cards or runes, and each card might have a different response or a different opinion on it about what to do. That's just one example, or you can use an object to help you with your intuition.

4) The fourth practice is contemplative intuitive practice. This exercise would be to pick an object, maybe it could be a stain glass window or a beautiful picture. And, you focus on it for a while. The object could be a crystal or special rock.

And, you observe it, and you look deeply at it, and you become receptive, and perceptive. And, you allow the feelings to come into you, and you allow the impressions and inspiration and ideas and intuition to flow to you. Doing this, you're somewhat in a trance state focusing on a particular object and nothing else, focusing on one object while avoiding all other things around you without distraction. And, that's the type of deep contemplation somewhat akin to Taizé meditation of the mystical Catholics. Almost all cultures have some type of iconic meditative practice.

5) And, number five would be just to read an affirmation or meditation and then to have some quiet time, and to allow thoughts and ideas and inspiration to come to you. I mentioned this before, but it could be a meditative book, or many people in different literatures have suggested that you just open a page in your favorite wisdom literature. It could be the Bible, Old Testament or New Testament. It could be some Native American, Vedic or Buddhist writings. It doesn't matter. And, you just open a page to it, you read it, and then meditate over that, and you allow, without distraction for your quiet time. To begin, it is sometimes best to take a few deep breaths, relaxed your body from head to toe, and you're able to go through this process of just allowing your mind to receive this beautiful information that comes from in and around the universe. With this practice you may have some aha moments from time to time which resolve long standing questions or challenges.

6) Number six, you can ask a question in the morning or in the evening, it doesn't matter. Let's say you ask a question in the morning of yourself like would it be good for me to move to Washington D.C., or London, it doesn't matter. And, you ask that question very quietly and very assertively to yourself in the morning in a relaxed way. And during that day, you look for signs. You look for signs and symbols from the universe that may guide you. And, let's say you're driving down the road that day, and you see a sign that says Washington or London or whatever it might be. Let's say that somebody starts talking about they had a great time while living at a certain place and you learn more. That's just an example of how you could ask a question and look for signs in your daily life.

7) And number seven, you write out ideas or questions that come to you mind and you keep writing them out on a scrap of paper. Let's say you write out, should I take this job, or should I move to this place, or should I invest in this investment, and you write these things down, you just keep writing out what comes to your mind. It could be anything. And, as you write these things out, maybe you'll see a ***pattern*** in the writing. And, that pattern on that page may,

the totality of the ideas may give you sign or a symbol or some path to take, or some way to act or not act. This may be especially effective with the type of work or hobbies that you seek. The overall pattern of ideas may point you to a type of work that you may master and become great at doing.

8) Another way to imagine doing something, a decision, imagine taking action in your life in some area, and then lock that idea in mentally and basically bring it down from your mind into your heart, almost like swallowing it, and feel this decision's impact on you and try to feel it in your heart, mind, and gut, but particularly in your gut.

So, you are imagine doing something like buying a house or a condo or a car, or moving to another place, or taking a job. You are imagining a new future event, you are imagining what it's like, imagining the outcome, and then you try to feel in your gut whether or not it is good or bad. Is it a yes or a no feeling?

And then you mentally turn on the computer in your mind and select the future time and date and result to see if the decision is beneficial or prevents harm, where it is not harmful. So, the key to this is really locking in some moment in the future, maybe a year from now, whatever, and just imagining what that future experience is like. It's got to be a little bit specific, but other than that, it's a good way to formulate the potentiality of a a yes or no feeling in your center of emotions and gut..

9) Object Holding Exercise – Sense the Energy

Another quick exercise would be maybe to hold an object that represents what the future might be and try and see if your imagination presents any ideas or events based on holding that object, whether you receive a little mental-movie clip or an idea that's running through your mind. This is yet another simple exercise to test your intuition or your inspiration.

10) The Papal Bowl of Intuition

Another exercise would be to cut out a couple of slips of paper and write on each slip of paper a particular action that you might take, or an object that you want or a type of car, it doesn't matter, and you are just writing three or four ideas on pieces of paper. You are sticking them in a bowl and you allow maybe one of your children to pick something from the bowl or a trusted friend. This is an idea that's been around forever. Even some of the popes in foreign lands are picked this way. In Egypt, the pope is selected by, they put three names of three Bishops in a bowl, and they allow a small child to pick one of the names out of the bowl and that's how the Pope is selected in the Coptic Church in Egypt.

In sum, this is a very existential practice of knowing yourself and trying to be your best and basically existentialism is really the freedom that lies where your authentic self is discovered.

In The Moment Intuition – Power of Inspiration

Wealth is a force for good, a force for learning, helps create experiences, funds expanded talents, and allows for expanded giving. In the essence of wealth, our reality is our acceptance of good. Success and prosperity and financial freedom is a reasonable option in life. Therefore, accepting the reasonableness and possibility of good in every moment is a present form or wealth consciousness.

Here are some Practice Steps to Harness Your Passions in Life

1. Take a moment to list the ideas that you have in the moment right now, and meditate on your objectives that you have. And then, listen to yourself and see what your thoughts are around your goals and objectives.

2. And then, mentally engage your idea, and then you can build upon the idea with action and allow innovation and improvisation.

3. What decision feels right? Use your gut without focusing on limited data. Change routines or do something differently, and empty yourself of your preconceptions.

4. What makes you feel alive? What is your passion? What would you do for free if you could do it?

5. How can you serve that will help the most people?

6. Earnestly commit to a full, free, and spiritual, and wealthy life.

7. Be good to yourself and know yourself and let go of your blocks and mental hindrances to your happiness.

8. Decide to believe and know that you can be what you want, do what you want and have what you want.

9. Define your mission. Who are you? What do you love to do? What do you want to be? What do you want to create? How will you serve? How will you create solutions for yourself and others?

10. Itemize what you want. See yourself using all of it. See yourself using all of the good that comes to you – the essence of your rewards and how you will use them for yourself and other people.

11. Empty yourself of mental thinking that keeps you from your dreams, and make room for growth, renewal.

12. Refocus on what is right with your world. Grow, change, learn, expand, experience, every penny you spend should be on growth, health and productivity.

13. Follow your heart, mind and soul, and take steps. Be aware and mindful, and use zeal in your life.

14. Revitalize yourself and be aware and engage life. Try and transform yourself into a rebirth, allow renewal, let go of your old views, study new ideas, expand new perspectives, become reborn in life, be aware of abundance, see abundance, try to see it in everything.

15. Develop a Prosperity Consciousness: See wealth, see prosperity, see beauty of nature, open your eyes to opportunity.

16. If you are going to engage life, you're going to have to think big, use big ideas, and find big solutions.

17. Action: And, once you have these big ideas, and solutions. You need to call people and act on these solutions, meet with others, communicate, connect to others

18. Deals: Get the deals done that are necessary to put all it altogether, get past your fear, get out of your comfort zone. And if someone says no, kick the dust off your sandals and move onto the next person.

19. Brand: You need to brand yourself and do all you can do to promote your ideas and solutions to the masses, and deliver the best and fastest service. If you can do all these things, you will be great.

Steps needed to Make Big Changes

1. The first would be desire.
2. Thought and imagery.
3. Open minded and awareness to change.
4. Planning.
5. Action.
6. Commitment to that action, and earnestness and sincerity.
7. Aim or what is your purpose.
8. Essence. The essence and what's in back of the purpose, such as emotions. And then how you devote your attention and what you are loyal to.
9. Remove or diffuse blocks and obstacles.
10. Connecting with the animating source, and develop a harmonious relationship with the Life Force.
11. Remaining grateful, thankful, and cultivate praise, both for yourself and other people.
12. Be aware of abundance and opportunity and goodness, and how your consciousness in all of that in sum is how your consciousness controls your destiny.

Exercises

Here are special observations for optimizing your consciousness. Consciousness through certain mental and physical, spiritual practices.

1. There is a collective consciousness and harmonic resonance, and how that affects the individual in their mind and memory. We have a stream of consciousness, and how that thought affects your consciousness in the 21st century, is the C2K. And then there is the spoken word and written word of effect in what you speak and what you write, and how that changes your consciousness going forward after you have made that mental imprint. And then there is controlled visualization, or controlled hypnagogia. Then there is autosuggestion, and how to use repetition in statements of affirmation and decrees to alter and enhance our ongoing mental stream of consciousness.

2. Our essence or being is altered by our thinking and your acting, and habits. Mindfulness, meditation and contemplation affects your consciousness. We can work at emptying or filling our mind with new information.

3. Then there are theories and ideas by greats such as Carl Jung who discussed archetypes and the imprints that are already within you, and what your types of passions, hobbies and work that you tend toward doing based on your archetype or what's in your background. In Vedic Hindu literature, there are many great writings about the energy of: purpose, dharma and even tapas.

4. One key exercise is to improve your consciousness through catharsis, purging, clearing, forgiving, cleansing of your mind and processing information, processing data. Just like a computer processor which has a memory, hard drive and temporary files and cache. We all realize these things need to be optimized to work together.. The same is true with the consciousness, and then there is spiritual energy that animates mind, and how that affects you. How spirituality affects a person.

5. The next exercise would be we have to advance in the type, quality, and nature of our dominant conscious thoughts. We have a choice in the type, quality, and nature of the dominant conscious thoughts that we have, and how do we change our thinking and alter the choices of our thoughts.

6. As an example in Philippians 4 it talks about how to choose what is true and beautiful and right, righteous and so forth. And that is a conscious choice

sometimes for many people where we use our power of: will or willingness to direct our thoughts to what is positive.

The Mind of Wonder and Awe

Awe and wonder are things that we perceive that are not typically in the five senses of taste, feel, smell, sound, and seeing, so we actually can experience something without a tangible comprehension. So, awe is also part of an extra-sensory perception, along with empathy as well. Since emotions are based on perception, there is something beyond the mere perception that causes a varying emotions.

The next section is about prayer and meditation, communing with the spirits and with God. A trance state, a meditative state, and the essence of the search for the Holy Grail is to maximize consciousness of life, abundance, aliveness, potential, and awareness. If we can operate from a higher order of perception, our view and journey are optimized. Further, a higher consciousness allows a greater connection prescience, and imagination, which can be utilized upon our inner and outer worlds. We have to be contemplative in action, and that is being connected to the universe, while being conscious of what is going on which, in essence, taps us into a higher grade of thought and insight.

In every culture there are different parts of the body from the crown at the top of your head to your heart to your throat down to your stomach and lower chakras and to your feet that ground you to the earth. All of these are interesting aspects of your body and yourself, which could be equated to aspects or facets of the soul as well.

Here is a short list of things or issues that may affect consciousness that may be beyond the normal 5 senses. Ways to alter consciousness and thinking.

1. There is the breath or the breath of life, and how the air itself you breath and the contents of that air can affect you and the quality of the air can affect you.

2. There are exercises and poses and different routines for the body to be stretched or strengthened.

3. There is nature and earth and how to commune with nature and the earth, whether it is outward bound or a vision quest, or anything else.

4. There are the five elements. How earth, wind, fire and ice, or a fifth element such as the all permeating ether that is in the interspaces of the universe.

5. The of course, diet and nutrition affects your consciousness and your perception of life.

6. There is also fellowship with others and whom you associate with, who you talk to, what you verbalize, what you hear and listen to—how that energy or vibration affects your consciousness.

7. Lists and objectives alter your consciousness. If you write a journal or make a list or add goals to the list, how does that change your focus and your intention, and how you put things in order in your life—the order in which they are important.

8. There are environmental issues, the people, the placed, and the things and the arrangement of energy and objects around you. Whether order changes your consciousness

9. The teacher and a guru relationship is an affect. If someone who is your trusted advisor, how does that affects your consciousness and your growth and your human potential.

10. How you speak is an affect. Your incantations and decrees, and affirmations and what you say and what you repeat out loud or in prayer, how that would affect your mental consciousness.

11. Applied meaning or your past. This raises the question of how your past or your childhood, and how your ancestors and elders all affects your karma, circumstances, luck, and your reaping and sowing of life.

12. How you utilize imagination and how to use exercises of imagination to expand your consciousness.

13. Neuroplasticity. Really about changing or reprogramming the way you think about your competencies.

14. Nootropics. How nutrition and diet and supplements, herbs and other types of regulated intake of chemicals can affect your awareness, function, consciousness, whether they are holistic chemicals or not.

I2K – Illumaniti C2K – Consciousness in the New Age –

15. Altered states; how some people are just born different. Some people were born really thinking in a vertical way or a horizontal way, and some people have visionary capacities, are more spatial in their mind. And some people who are a little on the edge of either autism or Asperger's or some type of bipolar issues. Sometimes those conditions can allow a person to think both logically, but more importantly in a non-logical way, which allows them to think outside of what the normal people are confined to.

16. Inner Gravity? And then the last issue is just the inner ear. How the compass or gravity of your inner body can affect you, and what that is. Everyone has an inner ear situation where it could be adjusted if necessary.

The Mystic Renaissance – Swedenborg to the 21st Century

One of the great esoteric writers of the Renaissance is Emanuel Swedenborg of Sweden. In his writings, it can be seen that he speaks of an alignment of consciousness.

To begin with, he advocates that you find your spiritual portal within you that connects you to the universal energy. For example, when you close your eyes and you meditate or become mindful, you will find that place within you where you feel super-consciously connected to the world.

Then, after you have meditated, you learn to seek your purpose and your passion or the things that you want or need to do.   And, you cultivate that intent, and you back it up with love energy, if you can.

Third, we begin to live rightly and put your spiritual lives first instead of your ego centric life, and try and live to the best of your ability in constructive ways, live rightly.

Fourth, we would be to maintain a simple faith in knowing just by using humility and compassion for others and for yourself. So, you've helped maintain your faith through humility and compassion.

Fifth, be good to others and to yourself.

And, these ideas ahve a lot to do with the golden rules such as: loving thy neighbor as thyself. As a note, if you look at the Bible and you look in the chapter in Luke.   the scribe or the lawyer says to Jesus that we need to love our neighbors as ourselves, and you need to do all you can to live up to your potential for the grace and glory of God.

As an example, sometimes, we'll watch a sporting event and we'll see someone win something, and they're very praiseful to the God of their understanding. A lot of people are living for the glory of the universe, and they're thankful for the potential that they have, and the talents that they've been given, and the ability that they've been given to cultivate those talents.

Timeless Principles of Success – Aurelius – Franklin – Sun Tzu

The pursuit of success is as old as civilization, and many ancient thought leaders promulgated lessons that are still relevant today. Below are some ideas from three of my favorite thinkers: Marcus Aurelius, Ben Franklin, and Sun Tzu.

Marcus Aurelius (121-180 AD)

Emperor Cesar Marcus Aurelius wrote the 12 Books of the Meditations as a source for his own guidance and self-improvement, and they have some great tips for business, spiritual balance, politics, and relationships. Much like the principles of the Art of War by Sun Tzu or Ben Franklin's 13 Virtues of character development, these insights from the warrior-general are designed to help the reader reach his or her potential. Marcus Aurelius was emperor of Rome and was notable among Roman emperors as he was a devotee to the study and practice of philosophy of Socrates, Plato, Alexander the Great and more. Here are the some Timeless Principles of Success from: Emperor Marcus Aurelius (all references are from *The Meditations of Marcus Aurelius*, translated by George Long. Vol. II, Part 3 of the Harvard Classics, New York: P.F. Collier & Son, 1909–14):

1.   Look for the best in life. (Book 10, §1)

2.   Acting with confidence and poise. (Book 3, §5)

3.   Be and live your purpose and focus upon engaging your vision and mission. (Book 9, §19 and Book 10, §16)

4.   Stay in the now and act in the present. (Book 8, §44)

5.   The present is a gift. (Book 8, §44)

6.   We must express ourselves naturally. Use your own style to be excellent but also use the most practical techniques. (Book 11, §13)

7.   Our greatest power is our choice and ability to control our thought - Choose not to be harmed and operate beyond the basic senses. (Book 4, §7)

8.	Go within to develop inner peace. Renew yourself, rest, meditate, and recharge. (Book 4, §3)

9.	Do your job with diligence, energy, focus and patience. (Book 3, §12)

10.	Be aware of the power within you and nurture it. This can include exercise, diet, rest, empowerment, and learning. (Book 2, §13)

11.	Projects can be broken down to tasks and achieved one at a time finishing each part with excellence. (Book 6, §26)

12.	Our every task is to be done in an excellent way and shine like a jewel of great wealth. (Book 7, §15)

13.	Be contemplative in action and listen to others to learn the best ways to respond. (Book 8, §5)

14.	No need to complain aloud or to yourself in mind. (Book 8, §9)

15.	The word attribute can mean to make a tribute, complement others' good works, and find acceptance and thankfulness outwardly. (Book 8, §23)

16.	Joy and memories are created. (Book 8, §25)

17.	Striving for the right view while repressing animal instincts (Book 8, §29)

18.	See past mere appearances. Try and go beyond what is apparent and see truth. (Book 12, §18)

19.	Focus on your purpose toward highest performance results while avoiding blame. (Book 12)

20.	Use what is available, maximize your talents, and take advantage of the things that are provided. (Book 8, §32)

21.	The imagination can lean toward negativity, but a constructive imagination in the now is very powerful. (Book 8, §36)

I2K – Illumaniti C2K – Consciousness in the New Age –

22.   Your soul takes the color of your thoughts. (Book 5, §16)

23.   Look at what you have, the things you value most and think how much you would crave them if you did not have them anymore. (Book 7, §27)

24.   Live your life as though today's actions will be remembered and you have one day left as a gift. Act and live without haste or sloth. (Book 7, §56)

25.   Change and impermanence are features of existence. Particularly that change is inevitable and that it should be embraced. (Book 9, §32)

26.   Give yourself time to learn something new and good, and cease to be whirled around. (Book 2, § 7)

27.   The Emperor stresses the importance to flow with the Universe and use its energy in your favor. (Book 8, §23)

Benjamin Franklin (1706-1790)

Benjamin Franklin was one of the founding fathers of the United States and was a leading author, politician, inventor, and diplomat. He sought to cultivate success and character in himself and others by using a methodology of thirteen virtues, which he developed in 1726 and continued to practice for the rest of his life. Franklin was a wise master, mystic, and much-loved ambassador. Franklin would reflect daily over his actions and character before going to bed in order to improve himself. Here is a customized version of Franklin's virtues of success (from *The Autobiography of Benjamin Franklin*. Philadelphia: H. Altemus, 1895):

1. "TEMPERANCE. Manage your behavior in a professional way."
2. "SILENCE. Speak with both purpose and skill, and only when needed."
3. "RESOLUTION. Resolve to perform with integrity and resolve."
4. "FRUGALITY. Invest in yourself and do not waste time."
5. CLEANLINESS. Respect of body, clothes, or home."
6. "MODERATION. Avoid extremes."
7. "INDUSTRY. Be engaged in activities that are purposeful; minimize unnecessary actions."
8. "SINCERITY. Be a constructive person who praises others; and, if you speak, speak professionally."
9. "JUSTICE. Keep your personal and business relations win-win where both parties benefit. Treat yourself and others with high regard
10. TRANQUILLITY. Be not distracted by the whims of society and focus on building your family, business and your customers.
11. "CHASTITY. Use your charisma in the right areas of your life."
12. "HUMILITY. Remain teachable and right sized."
13. "ORDER. Keep healthy routines with body, mind and spirit. Use planning to focus on building your character and helping people in each key area of their lives."

Sun Tzu (544-496 BC)

Sun Tzu was a Chinese general who is credited with *The Art of War*, a military strategy guide. Its principles are written broadly enough that many of them still apply to non-military struggles today. Below are some of Sun Tzu's timelessly relevant maxims, modernized for today's strategic risk management battles (from Lionel Giles' edition of *The Art of War* by Sun Tzu, 1910, Public Domain):

a) **Laying Plans/The Calculations**

Use a SWOT analysis for any situation or client. Look at the strengths, weaknesses, opportunities and threats for any challenge or situation.

b) **Waging War/The Challenge**

Know what you are willing to invest in each situation and know when move on to the next option or plan.

c) **Attack by Stratagem/Planning Offense**

All relationships should have a vision and mission. You should know what you will say, how to say it, know the environment, and be prepared to answer tough questions.

d) **Tactical Dispositions/Positioning**

Each of us should know the options, choices and alternative for each unique situations to provide skill and diligence into our activities.

e) **Energy/Directing**

Use your personal energy and charisma to help people but also allow your team to assist you in any way that will allow you to be a success.

f) **Weak Points & Strong/Illusion and Reality**

Each client's situation, business, and family dynamic changes with time. Be prepared to assist customers with each new season by maintaining knowledge about your key customers.

g) **Maneuvering and Dealing with Confrontation**

Be prepared for tough people, tough family members, children, spouses, and other non-traditional relationships. Empower decision makers to work with you.

h) **Variation in Tactics/The Nine Variations**

Be prepared to respond to shifting circumstances successfully.

i) **The Army on the March/Adapting**

With new laws and new government rules, all of us must stay apprised of the best education and information using our awareness.

j) **Terrain/Situational Positioning**

Know your surroundings and people. Communicate with them the information they need to make informed decisions or utilize the benefits that you offer.

I2K – Illumaniti C2K – Consciousness in the New Age –

k) **The Nine Situations/Nine Terrains**

Understand the terrains of Life, Relationships, Health, Success, Business, Wealth, Mind, Consciousness, and Peace.

l) **The Attack by Fire/Fiery Attack**

Use strategic tactics: Marketing, Time Management, Planning, Management, and more.

m) **The Use of Intelligence**

Competitive intelligence and benchmarking allow you to know your competition, know your customer, and know your target market.

Abundance Prosperity & Success Techniques

Throughout life, there is always a celebrated group of people who succeed and many of us who fail. What separates the two groups? As an avid reader of success literature and research, there are many psychological, human potential, and even metaphysical strategies advocated to improve your performance or reinvigorate your potential. The irony to life is that we will all need to grow, improve, and change our character and capabilities in just about any career that we engage in.

To begin this discussion, let us start with the premise that all great businesses begin with an idea. Many businesses are successful by the use of great planning; thus, thoughts can turn into real things. Your thoughts combined with the appropriate desire and plans are the basis of most success.

A strong desire is usually what can bring your idea into a reality. So, if you began your business idea with the strong desire to grow and never look back, you probably are successful if you had the persistence to continue through the inevitable cycles of growth.

All of us began with some sort of plan of action to grow our business. Some of us had very detailed plans and others did not. Planning is crucial because most people do not define what they will do and are too timid to write down exactly what they want to achieve and how they will realize the goal in any degree of specificity.

Thus, having definite objectives and a specific plan along with a strong desire for success is generally what is needed to accomplish great things. Here are some attributes of winners: A burning desire is something that you really want to do. You are willing to take action on your burning desire and develop an action plan. You should have faith that you can make your plan happen. You are willing to sever the past and move forward with your objectives and desires. You are willing to focus your attention and positive emotions almost exclusively on this career project, and never give up. Having your stated objectives while engaging positive thoughts, enthusiasm, and persistence that is built on honesty and integrity will propel your business growth.

In this next section, there are clear bullet points that describe an easy exercise to define your plan. This involves putting pen to paper. On paper, you will write out clearly what you want to achieve.

How to Create a Personal Agreement with Yourself by Firmly Establishing What You Want. Write Your Plan in Specific Terms by Determining:

· What you desire to accomplish (the amount of clients or dollars under management or annual salary)
· What service, time commitment, and value that you will give to earn and deserve the outcome
· How you will conduct and arrange your life and business to allow the receipt of prosperity and compensation.
· The date your goal will be achieved.
· Sign and date the written plan or contract with yourself
· Read the plan daily upon beginning your workday and before retiring for the evening.
· Frequently feel that you have achieved success in heart and mind and harvest that emotion of attainment.
· Imagine what you will do with your success after you acquire success.

Enthusiasm and Faith can be induced through several practices or exercises: Enthusiasm and a proactive attitude are some of the major forces that when coupled with your desire can propel a plan. As for the Metaphysical Aspect of Success:

Relax Technique

Many professionals use this technique for a few minutes a day to reaffirm their personal faith and success mentality so that they will indeed accomplish what they desire.

· Find a quiet spot to relax
· Read statements of desire (think about your personal objectives in you minds eye)
· Practice forming mental images of your personal success in your spare time.
· Project the image of your success on the subconscious mind using a heart felt emotion. See that you have success already in your imagination: For example, imagine yourself with a salary 5 times what it is today and feel the emotions of achieving that goal at year-end. We stress that you do this daily.
· Engage Affirmations by reading aloud the professional and successful attributes that you desire such as: "I am a great professional and deserve to have great clients. (OR you should read your personal agreement statement frequently)

I2K – Illumaniti C2K – Consciousness in the New Age –

· Use gratitude and thankfulness of heart. As many success writers state, "Complaining and being negative is a waste of your time and energy". Moreover, when being thankful for your job, career, clients, health and so forth, you will create an energy of attraction that will bring you more positive outcomes, happiness, and success. Further, new clients and your existing clients will be more attracted to your successful and positive outlook. Believe me, clients can sense this. Therefore, you should contemplate the good in your life while relaxing and having a sense of well-being.
· Combine the above with Action, Action and More Action See Below.

As for a Successful Action Plan

· Your actions must be persistent. This means that we should be proactive in building new business as well as keeping satisfied customers.
· Avoid lack of decision and procrastination, and stick with your decision and plan. An example of this would be to let go of a bad client, if managing this relationship is consistently abusing your time and energy without just rewards and payment for your time.
· Write down each day what you will do to move forward with your business plans. Be efficient and effective. Do all you can do each day without haste. Do not worry about yesterday or tomorrow. Today, you should accomplish all you can. Over time, this adds up, and you will receive positive results in your business.
· Strong thoughts of gratitude and enthusiasm will bring about change for the better in you and your environment. This simply means to focus what you desire and on being the best and thinking about the best for you, your family, and your business.
· Organize your affairs so that you can receive the rewards of a better business. Thus, allow for new and better clients. Believe that you deserve them. Do not be afraid to charge them value for value. This may mean acquiring greater business tools, administrative assistance, infrastructure use, and ways to capture income. This may entail offering a broader line of products or services. In any event, be prepared to provide solutions and do the homework before asking for the free lunch.
· Surround yourself with encouraging professional mentors or advisors.
· Know in your heart that an outcome similar to what you expect or something even better will come to you at the right time.

Professional Growth and Mentor Groups:

· Develop a group of friends who can give you professional insight and feedback and will support your goals and share their own personal experiences and success tactics.
· You should be willing to help all members in this group of professional friends with your knowledge, skill, and support.
· Meet often for planning and to obtain and give feedback to your group.
· You must always speak and act to maintain harmony with this group with positive and encouraging conversation. Thus, never belittle or constantly contradict your group members. Offer solutions, not criticism.

Belief in Yourself, Your Products and Service:

Believe that your products and services are as good or better than any products out there. Know the details of your products and services. Be able to articulate the benefits of your service. Chances are that what you sell is just as good as what the competition offers. Your products and services create opportunity for clients. Do not be afraid to sign up the new business client because someone else will do this if you don't. Moreover, remember that some small clients take just as much time to manage as very large clients. Therefore, time management is essential. As they say, "Over time, it is better to have 20 great accounts than 150 non-productive customers."

Affirmative & Constructive Action

 Taken as a whole, it is impossible for anyone to achieve their goals, their objectives and their dreams without proficient <u>action</u>. How does anyone begin one thing and complete it? Keep in mind, every task has to begin with some act of boldness. As the famous Von Goethe stated, every idea or plan has to be begun, and once you take that first step, you have taken an action towards the completion of that goal or attainment of that dream. So each day we have to do all we can to achieve that particular goal. We have to do all we can in the present moment and stay focused one step at a time, towards the incremental achievement of a particular objective. And I think that's what people mean by the concept of "24 hours a day". You don't have yesterday, you don't have tomorrow; what you have is today. All we have is right now and it's a gift, and if you can focus your mind and your attention on the actions that you need to do now and get them done effectively and efficiently, then you are destined to become great and destined to have a richer and fuller life.

I2K – Illumaniti C2K – Consciousness in the New Age –

If you don't know how to begin, take out a pen and paper and write down three things that you can do tomorrow, the three most important things that you can do tomorrow towards the attainment of your dream. And if you can't do all three tomorrow, it doesn't matter. But remember, each day you can do three things, for the betterment of yourself and the betterment of your family and the betterment of society. And at the end of the day, if you do three things a day, you will have done over 1,000 actions in one year towards making yourself a better person, developing self-regard, building yourself up from the inside out, and at the end of one year, believe me, people will know the difference. And with writing, this habit imprints ideas on the sub-conscious to work on and sort out both while awake and sleeping. Thus, the process of writing tasks embeds the action plan in the mind so that it becomes a purpose-backed desire to work on or at the least, to think about.

Being Successful

In my career, I have helped many people. I feel great joy in contributing to anyone's financial freedom. Moreover, I realize that many of you are great successes already and commend all of you. With success, there is usually hard work and many people who depend on you. As a reminder, there will be times when you just need to rest, relax, or take a vacation. There will be seasons where you may need to rejuvenate your enthusiasm for your business. With all of that being said, you physical and mental wellbeing is the most important thing to maintain so that you may continue all of your good works. Therefore, try to keep a balance with body, mind and soul and incorporate good exercise, diet, leisure, and rest with your professional life.

Further Self Analysis Exercises to Free the Mind.

A good exercise is to write out the things that have cause us great discomfort, resentment, anger, and so on. Self analysis can appear difficult. Further, we would really rather just make a list of all of the persons that kept us from getting our way or caused us harm. It would be much easier to just make a blame sheet that explains why we feel uncomfortable with others or ourselves.

However, blame is not the point. We should take a hard look at our life. What did we do to facilitate our problems? What was our part? What were the raw feelings? By the way, some people have suggested to be sure and list things that you like about yourself while doing this exercise. That was a good suggestion because I make a "what I like about myself list" occasionally, and I am reminded how well the Universe is taking care of me. The bad stuff should be aired, vented, and cleared away with the proper people or friends. The good stuff can be cleaned, refined, expanded, and grown while new ideas are allowed in. Naturally, a healthy self-esteem can be good for the spirit, attitude, and faith.

To make a long story short, we can find somebody to listen. We should schedule a sufficient block of time. We prepare a list in advance to discuss. We spend as much time as needed to work through the personal history to another trusted person who is sympathetic to our growth. We should probably not to glorify a retched past. By the way, most people feel a great deal better after this excercise. Some people do keep a few things to themselves that they do not want the listener to know. Soon thereafter, most people may find a professional person to discuss the sensitive issues with. Overall, this process can be like a fountain cleansing our soul.

To some, this process may seem like a miracle. We are free again, and we now understood a strategy to stay free. Discuss it, diffuse it, and give it away to the power of the universe. Begin anew with constructive thinking. One of the golden keys to happiness and great success is the way you interpret events that unfold before you. Highly successful people are master interpreters. People who have attained greatness have a amazing ability in this area. They have the spiritual skill to interpret negative events as positive challenges that will assist them in growing and moving even farther up the ladder of success. Some of the masters can turn rejection into healthy challenges or failure into being guided into a safe direction. Remember, no one can insult without your permission.

Magical Guided Meditation – Consulting Your Holy Self

Step 1 - Before you go into any guided meditation, you should relax the body top to bottom and go into the alpha state which is the condition of a Relaxed Mind and Body.

Focus your relaxation on each part of the body. Start with your toes and go all the way up through your legs and to your knees and hips and into your body. And take a deep breath and into your lungs and feel your heart beating and let it go all the way to the tips of your fingers and the tips of your toes and allow your body to relax. And all the way to the top of your head, to your mind and your eyes, and then to your crown, and just connect yourself all there is.

That's the first step.

To be in a relaxed position, you can be sitting in a chair or lying down, which are probably the best two positions. It is probably not a good idea to do this while in the car, while I do believe that some of the advanced souls can be driving and do these exercises without a problem.

For beginners, it's best to do it in a quiet spot where you're not distracted. This as a directed exercise, you imagine yourself as your favorite animal for instance. It could be a lion, a falcon, an eagle, a tiger or bear, or it could be your favorite dog or cat. Imagine yourself as that animal traveling through the tranquil forest, or flying over a peaceful forest or lake. As you see a large fortress or castle, you enter into that sacred space. As you approach the fortress or the castle the doors open for you. You arrive there as the animal you are, and then you transform back into your warrior self.

Imagine a medieval castle and imagine your clothes being medieval armor and you walk into the castle, and as you walk into the great hall there is someone there at the end of the hall on a throne, and you walk up to that throne, and as you look at the person who is up there, you have a great realization. IT is in fact you, and you decide to have a conversation with your holy, royal self.

And you ask questions, questions you've always wanted to ask yourself about what you should do, where you should travel one day. You can ask anything such as, what type of life you should have or what type of purpose you should live. What type of mission you should have in your life. What type of things you should create, what types of things you should go for.

Whatever it might be, and this holy self will have a voice. A voice similar to yours, but it is NOT yours. It is a different but Authentic voice that is connected to the source of all good. It is the voice that can guide you, and give you peace, and give you direction, and when you finish discussing these things with your holy self. Thank your Holy Self. You can give the person a name if you want. It can be a man or a woman, even if it's not you, it can be someone of a different gender and still be you. But it represents you, and you thank your higher self for all the help and as you walk away, you close the door behind you knowing you can return at anytime.

You transform back into that part of your soul that is a mighty being or peaceful animal, and you come back to your home and body where you are in your imagination.

In most cases you would open your eyes and you'd be back of course in your own reality. And you could take out a pen and paper and write notes, think about the experience, and then maybe try it again sometime soon.

I want to encourage everybody to do this but keep in mind that you want to make sure that when you are traveling to this special place that it's at a peaceful time, that it's a peaceful journey, and take a few deep breaths and as you travel to this sacred shrine to visit your Holy Self, whether it be a castle or a fortress or anywhere, you want to make sure that your journey there is peaceful and serene, and that when you arrive there you are ready to have a meaningful discussion.

And that's about it for this particular exercise.

Spiritual Exercises with Magical Power

1. Basic Prayers for Memory

The first practice is basic prayers. An example of a basic prayer might be the Serenity Prayer by Reinhold Niebuhr: "God grant me the serenity to accept the things I cannot change, the courage to change the things I can, and the wisdom to know the difference." Many other prayers are perfectly acceptable for all types of spiritual seekers. Many of us use the Sermon on the Mount, which includes the Lord's Prayer or "Our Father".

2. Fellowship Exercise

The next activity is seeking wise counsel and fellowship. One of the top types of spiritual practice in the 21st century (also in the 20th century) is seeking out other spiritually minded people who want to grow and heal in a spiritual way. There are two parts to this—you are giving of yourself and you are letting others give to you. For instance, you may be going to a spiritual gathering where you could discuss wisdom literature, the Bible, or some other spiritual literature and sharing your experience about it, sharing your interpretation of it, sharing your strength and hope regarding the discussion or mentoring or counseling or coaching or sponsoring other people. The reward to this is you are giving it away, but you are also teaching it. You are teaching about something even as you are learning about something. Therefore, you are giving it away to keep it. If you give of yourself, invariably, you are receiving the rewards of the universe by trying to help other people who are deeply in need.

3. Active Meditation

Active meditation involves reading certain meditative literature, absorbing what it means, musing over the literature, thinking about it, and discussing it with other people out loud. Sometimes when you have an active meditation for reading it could be something written like a psalm or a proverb or a Bible passage. You may even have a dictionary available to interpret each word amongst other people, and then you discuss it out loud, but you can read it out loud as well before discussing it. To give you an example, some people may be sitting on a train, maybe reading an article in the newspaper and they put the newspaper down and think about it for several minutes and just allow their body to absorb the information and muse over it and then discuss it later. That's an example of active meditation. And a lot of people think they don't have the ability to meditate, but really most people do because if you just show up somewhere for a spiritual discussion you are in the process of actively meditating over something with other people.

4. Seeking Inspiration

The next section is praying for inspiration as a practice. That is when you can either sit down by yourself and get into a relaxed state and ask the universe for ideas or answers, for God's will, for the ability and the strength to do the right thing, and that's what we mean by praying for inspiration or seeking inspiration. One of the truths about inspiration is, you don't have to act on it; you can seek wise counsel about the inspiration that you've received and ask if it's a good idea. Or, you can just run it through a generalized litmus test. Is the idea or is the inspiration something that will help other people, or something that will be unselfish and loving and good for your heart and your mind? Those are things to ask yourself when you seek inspiration and when you decide to act on the inspiration.

5. Seeking God Consciousness

The next section is praying for the presence of the universe and praying for the presence of God. This includes praying for the energy of God and the spirit of the universe to be with you, to be conscious of it, and to cultivate a God-consciousness. Next, you can seek to develop a harmonious relationship with your universe and with your God and to be at peace with yourself, other people, and with nature. Ultimately, if you can ask for all these things and be open to perceiving them, you will actually find that you have developed a consciousness of love of yourself and the world around you. That is the ultimate goal of most orthodox practitioners of spirituality, and that goal is unity and non-separateness, a unity with your authentic self and unity with God and the world.

6. Mass as a Sacrament

The next section is mass as a sacrament. What people overlook is many orthodox spiritual practitioners carry out the ritual of attending a temple or a church or a cathedral or some spiritual house. For the people who attend those services and rituals, those activities are a sacrament, a sacred act. Included in many rituals are singing, chanting, and praying, supplicating, and even circumambulating—a word I like to use that means "walking around." It also refers to the ritual movement of people, whether it be a priest, a rabbi, or other religious leader—the movement of people in a sacred space, asking for and invoking the power and presence of the supernatural into that place of worship—that is a sacrament. The circumambulation, the movement, is certainly a part of the spiritual practice, participating in it, being part of it, and seeing it. Many people actually participate in it by either singing or being part of a choir or being part of the group on the altar that does certain things, and they don't have to be priests, they can just be helping out. So, that is actually a very high orthodox practice.

7. **Absorption Exercise:**

The first principle is called absorption and it is about how in Mother Nature plants and animals absorb what is around them. They are able to take in the nutrients, food, and sunlight that they need to grow and to be healthy. As human beings and spiritual beings, one of our primary jobs is to learn to absorb the beneficence of the universe, to absorb what is good around us. That includes the sunlight and the trees and the fresh air and the wonderful scents and aromas that we smell in our environment and the sounds and the noises and the animals and the wildlife and the mountains and the beaches to see it, to feel it, to absorb it, to take it in. This is about learning how to pause and take a deep breath and really draw in life's energy, draw in life's energy. The flip side of that is we need to be able to learn to strategically avoid things that rob us of our energy or steal from us without our permission. I know that's not always possible, but we can strategically avoid toxic situations, toxic people, and toxic encounters and avoid escalating situations where the problem can only get worse. Remember that nine out of ten times great miracles can happen when we just walk away and keep our mouth shut, and there is a time and a place for all of us to stand up for ourselves with or against other situations, issues, or people. But in general, and we need to know, you know, when you are in the presence of another person close your eyes and test how you feel around that other person. Are they taking energy from you? Is there a kindred spirit? Do they help you grow? Do they support you? Do they sustain you? This is not only people, but it can be places and things as well.

With this law of absorption you may need to take a few minutes each morning or each evening before you go to bed, close your eyes and take a few deep breaths and relax each part of the body, and then just consciously think to yourself of what is good in the universe, what good happened to you during the day, what blessings happened. Take some time to think about those people who have been good to you over your lifetime and try and feel that goodwill that came to you, feel that love that someone gave to you in the past. It could be your spouse or your aunt or your uncle, your mother, your father or your brother, your sister, or a teacher. Just think of that one person who gave you love and try to be thankful for that in your heart and in your mind. And remember that each day that supply surrounds us, abundance surrounds us—the air, the water, the life. But we must be open in our heart and in our mind to receiving freely of this supply.

8. Willingness Exercise:

The next section is about willingness. What kind of willingness is good and healthy? What kind of willpower is good and healthy? The short answer is that when you decide and allow yourself to do something and you take that first step of action, you become willing by moving in the direction of your ideas and your dreams. But the real tough part of it is that you have to learn to exert your will. In doing so, you draw yourself closer to the abundance of the universe and closer to your GOD. , To be willing you have to be able to persist. You have to believe and accept that your goal is possible. Many writers have said the idea wouldn't even be in your mind if it wasn't possible. For many of us it's just difficult to accept and take life's abundance and reach our hands out and let the gift be put in our hands. One famous author used to begin his presentations by holding up $100 bill and saying, "Who wants $100?" It could be a crowd of 1,000 people and finally after 10 or 20 seconds usually one person would finally jump out of their chair and run up there and grab the money. That's the way we have to look at life and sometimes we have to just get up and make our move and take what life is offering us and meet life halfway. Meet Mother Nature halfway. Meet your god and your maker and your creator halfway. Meet the spirit of the universe halfway.

9. Give it Away Exercise:

The next little idea is we have to give it to keep it and to learn it to be able to teach it and to be able to tithe in divine ways. We have to be able to give of ourselves the best of ourselves to the universe and the universe will continue to give to us. It doesn't mean you have to donate all your time to charity or donate all of your money to charity, but it does mean that when you are helping others with your spare time or doing the best to support your family and your children, it has a ripple effect on your life and humanity in general. You know, the better you learn to take care of yourself the better you can take care of others. If you learn to take care of your family, you know society will help take care of you.

10. Character Building Ritual

The next section is character and building character. The thing we have to remember is that our character is what creates our vibration, and our vibration is what attracts things to our life. We have to continue to build our character and that means adding things to our lives that are good for us on a body, mind, and spirit level. And we have to improve those things, while letting go of the things that hold us back and keep us down. This means letting go of the bad habits that keep us from heading in the direction of our dreams. So, our character attracts the same type of energy to us just like two tuning forks vibrate at the same level. It's a type of resonance. It's how we radiate our good feelings. If we radiate vibrations of excellence and advancement and improvement, people will be attracted to us. When people sense we are giving more to life than we are taking from it, the want to do business with us or even have relationships with us.

Sometimes I counsel people whose lives are in a rut and they are trying to make some big changes are stuck, and I always tell them to be careful about getting into a relationship at this time. You have a better chance of making life changes if you are not trying to develop a new relationship, and likewise, you will be available for a meaningful relationship once you get your inner house in order. A person who is going to the gym, taking care of their body and going to school, taking care of their mind, or taking on a new job and getting new skills, will become more attractive to other people.

The next thought is just about your purpose. All of us have to find meaning in life, and we have to pick a purpose. We have to dedicate ourselves to something and choose the direction we want to go in. This could be choosing big goals or a five- or ten-year goal, or it could just be a one-day goal. In any event, you have to pick something. You have to commit to different activities. We have to commit to different tasks and goals and we have to find our purpose. Purpose for us is what you above all want to accomplish, either today or for the rest of your life. Maybe you can't figure that out right now, but at least write it down this question: "What do I really, really want to do, dedicate myself to?" Maybe it could be some niche idea or topic of study or research, just what do I want to specialize in, or what do I want to be the best at? Once you find that goal and you are ready to go forward and never look back—that's usually what defines greatness. People who can pick something and stay focused on it can become great in that particular area if they are willing to commit to it and dedicate their lives to it and never look back.

11. Awareness Exercise:

This next paragraph is about awareness, and for us to be aware we need to wake up. We need to wake up in our minds. We need to see truth regardless of appearances and we need to lose our sense of separateness from the world and allow ourselves to be part of it and to see it, to feel it, to interact with it and be more and more aware of our surroundings. When we do this, we can become saturated with the idea that there is abundance and prosperity in this world.

12. Association Exercise:

The law of association is about the principle that the energy that you associate with are what you will become. The more time you spend with somebody or the more you are in a certain type of environment, the more one you are going to become one with it and the more you are going to identify with a certain group of people, a certain place, or certain types of things.

13. Creativity:

The next section is creativity. All of us are born with a certain creativity, a certain type of expression. We have to learn to express ourselves and express that God-given talent and learn to express it at the highest level we can. It could be little ideas, it could be little bits of creativity, it could be making little pieces of art, writing little poems, creating special clothing, or making little arts and crafts that people want. Every one of us have our own desires to express ourselves and be our authentic selves and express our authentic purpose. What I'm trying to say to you is that unless we head in the direction of our creativity and use our hands and our minds and our bodies we may become frustrated in life that we are not participating in our ideas and our creativeness that belongs to us.

14. Spiritual Gymnasium

The next thing is about mental and spiritual strength, and I do believe many of us need to continue in the spiritual gymnasium everyday to continue in that prosperity and abundance workout every day. If you can cultivate a prosperity consciousness that becomes so strong that you are easily able to harvest abundance, then you will have developed real spiritual strength. You have to learn to be so strong as to deny and refute the endless possibilities of something not going your way because it's very easy for us to sit around and say, oh, this is going to happen, this bad is going to happen, or this is not going to go my way. It's so easy to be a nega-holic. But by the same token, if you can focus your mind at looking at all of the possibilities of greatness and wealth and abundance and creativity, then you will be immune from the sickness of negativity.

15. Sacred Days

The next section is about the sacred days, which could include various holidays: Christmas or Easter, St. Joseph's Day, All Saints/Red Mass, 12th Night, or even May Day. Many of these sacred days are based on the lives of Saints, the lives of the masters or, of course, seasonal festivities. Participation in these festivities may call for different rituals, different types of altars, different types of songs, different types of vestments and attire. Some even have a Festival of Saints, for instance, Semana Santa.   People in Spain dress up in special outfits and carry large candles and they have different marching groups, and they go through the town. In some of these cities and towns, whether it be Germany or Austria or Span, have these sacred festivals. Some of them are hundreds of years old. They're even in different parts of Germany. They have carnival days which some people call Drei Tolle Tage or Three Crazy Days that goes back almost 800 years as it relates to Carnival Karneval. These are sacred days. These festivities allow people to fellowship and congregate and celebrate certain times of the year. Some people even were able to unwind and relax as a by-product of these festivities. And other types of festivities allow them to enter sacred meditation, sacred prayer, sacred communion with either a spiritual master or holy person like the Mother Mary.

16. Services and Sacred Space

Another type of ritual is praying the stations of the cross, fasting, or even communion itself. In any of these cases, you may be invoking the Spirit of the Universe, God, or Christ, Mother Mary, or some other master and invoking the presence of that master into your life. And you may also engage in certain types of fasting or dietary restrictions as a symbol of sincerity. With communion and during masses and liturgies, the priests are invoking the presence and the actual energy of God into the alter and congregation, and they're administering that sacred energy or communion to individuals to help unite them with the Holy Spirit as well as remove their sins and help protect them from wickedness.

17. Nature Bound and Pilgrimages and Commitments

The next type of ritual is a retreat or a time-out or a visit with nature, or even a committed rehabilitation of some sort. There are people who actually take vows with a certain organization perhaps as a monk or an oblate. These are different types of specialized higher rituals with higher degrees of commitment. I've know many families who go on annual retreats together. Some of them are quiet retreats. Some of them are active retreats where they're at a place and eating with others. This type of communal activity is a way to get quiet and relax and get back to the roots of your faith and your life and help draw closer to God and nature. Another example might be a pilgrimage of some sort, such as a hadj or people in Europe that are traveling to a holy place. Some people go to holy places of healing and ask for healing, whether it be in France or Germany or Jerusalem or wherever. In Japan there's these holy places that people go to so they can seek out the energy. Some people refer to these holy places as energy centers. If you've ever been to the top of a pyramid, say in Central America, and felt the energy of that, you would know exactly what I'm talking about. An example of that would be the pyramid in Tepotzlan, Mexico where you can crawl to the top of the mountain. It's a fantastic little way to commune with nature and the heavens. There's actually steps that go up to the top of that mountain.

18. Retreats

Now another facet of a retreat would be an individual type of retreat. If you look at the old Celtic, Viking, and Norse literature, there were people there that would go sitting. They would do what is called sitting out and commune with themselves. They invoke the presence of nature and they would seek out the inspiration and guidance of the Fetch, which would be the animal part of their soul. Some people relate most to a lion or a bear or an eagle. You can go out into nature and commune with whatever animal part of your nature that you feel closest to. It's different than the clan part of your soul that they call the Sippe. The Fetch, the part of your animalistic part of your soul, is what some people also consider your guardian angel. Many people consider that they have a guardian angel. In some other cultures, that guardian is believed to be an actual animal itself or that animal part of your soul, which is fascinating. Some people refer to that in mystical books as the elemental body.

So, these are various types of things you can do to commune with yourself and nature and God: retreats, rehabilitation and sitting out, pilgrimages, and taking in nature, or a nature trip. All of these are ways to get closer to God and to yourself and to Earth.

19. Catharsis and Purification

Around the world, regardless of culture and spirituality or tribe, there are groups that form different purification rituals. These rituals could be done when a baby is born or comes of age to be baptized. Purification could be done through either water or submersion into water, or it could be done through the application of an ointment **** or smoke. If you've ever seen Native Americans, sometimes they can smudge a person or blow smoke on them to purify them and their body or purify a room. That's just an example of clearing. In the Celtic and Viking literature you'll see different types of magical clearing of space where they perform clearing of an area. They could clear to the north and the south and the east and the west. The geographical points, of course, were in the upper and the lower, you'll see that in ****, Native American seven-direction type exercise. So the purification is good from culture to culture to culture.

What I find interesting is that in the ancient world, including India, purification involves two things, and all catharsis and cleansing and emptying, but in the ancient literature it also included a filling and I think filling is one of the most overlooked aspects of spiritual catharsis and cleansing and purification. Let's say you've been through a tough life and you've had some fears and resentments and some angers and some ideas related to the past that you want to let go; there are two ways to do it. You can try to empty yourself and let go of those issues, those ideas and thoughts, but you can also start filling your mind and your heart with new ideas, new affirmations, new decrees, new empowerments, and new ways of thinking. That also leads to new habits and new actions. Our character is about the totality of our thinking and action and omissions, three different areas; but if you are able to develop new thinking and new habits, you can affect your character. So, developing new ideas, forming new beliefs, and forming new habits, that's really a process of magic that changes us at the core of our being. It changes our DNA structure and it changes our neural pathways, all of that is augmented and changed. And even our future is changed as a by-product of it because if you can continue to clear yourself and add only what's good for you and healthy for you into your life, it affects your life moment to moment and into the future as well. Because if you continue to do good things in the moment then many times it has a ripple effect into the future and with what you think each day in the way you wake up each morning.

20. Contemplative Action

The next spiritual practice is to become contemplative in action. That means to become mindful of the universe while you are engaging in life's activities, not only mindful but connected to the energy of the universe. Connected to the positive source, which most people call God, so you're connected and contemplative while in action. You're mindful while you're working, and you're connected to that perfect energy. One of the keys to being mindful is to be more aware while you are connected.

So, you're trying to do the right thing, while also being more aware of your surroundings at any given moment, more aware of what's going on inside you. More aware of what's going on outside of you. With that higher awareness, with that higher connection, you're operating at a higher level, and you're not missing out on the signs and symbols and miracles of life, and the gifts that come to you and the people that are sent to you. All of that is extremely important when remaining contemplative in action. It's like being in a meditative state while being active at the same time.

21. Daily Meditations and Daily Prayers

The next section is about daily liturgy and morning and evening prayers and seasonal prayers. Regardless of what faith and spirituality you are there's probably some good books that can help you in developing your daily meditations, your daily prayers, your daily devotions. All of this is there to help you get into the alpha state, get into the meditative state each day, and become connected to your world and become at peace with yourself and other people. Take a few deep breaths and really prepare for your day, and take time in the evening to prepare to go to sleep, and see if you can be a better person in the next day.

Now, daily liturgy can also mean just a book that you read and meditate over when you're doing your daily prayers. Many people also attend a daily service or an evening or morning mass they could go to with a few people, and that way they're able to pray and commune with each other. They have a little service where they're able to ask for help, and ask for forgiveness, and for empowerment to be of service to the world and to their family.

22. Meditative Objects

The next section is about icons and prayers cards and meditative objects and services. This is very interesting. I don't know if you've ever walked in on a maze, a spiritual maze, and taken the steps according to the actual little walk and made the prayers in each little section of the maze, but that's just an example of a prayer type of activity related to yourself, and to the given place. The other thing is with icons, you may have little icons on your desk or in your home that remind you of a spiritual master or a god or a holy mother or Buddha or whatever it might be. The point of that is just to recognize and be able to have that consciousness or higher power.

Prayer cards are something smaller. Of course, you can keep them in your wallet or in your purse and they may have a beautiful picture on one side and a prayer on the other side. And it's something you can hold and physically look at and pray. If there's a special prayer on one side for protection or whatever, it could be a saint on the card, or it could be Jesus Christ, it could be Lakshmi, the goddess of progeny and abundance from India, it doesn't matter. The point being is that it's a physical object that allows you to stay connected. You're not worshipping the object. You're just using it as a reminder and a mental refresher of your commitment to being spiritually connected. In addition, there are services that are less liturgy oriented, and they're more meditative oriented. If you've ever been to a Taize service, you'll understand that it's a type of meditative service in a regular Christian Church where you try and meditate on an object and an idea in quietude.

23. Spiritual Jewelry and Charms

Another type of personal ritual and practice that many people have is just the collection of spiritual things to wear whether it be a necklace or a bracelet, or something to hold in your pocket or a keychain, or it could be anything like that or some type of medallion. **** I'm sure some people may even use an earring or some other type of ring, but that's beside the point. I'm not really talking so much about charms and amulets. I'm mainly talking about reminders, reminders of protection and the power of protection, and the power of blessings that you may want to carry with you or wear on your body.

An example would be the cross of St. Benedict. It's a fantastic cross, and it has the Latin words inscribed up and down the cross that a lot of people don't know, but it says "The cross will protect me that goes before me" on one side of it, and on the other side of the cross it says that "No demon will be able to get me." So, it's kind of a fantastic little charm that goes back probably 300 or more years which is really amazing in one particular faith. And that's just one example of a type of charm or a cross that is carried by certain people.

24. Energy Centers

The next section is about holy places or sacred places, for example a temple, a Hindu temple, or a mosque in a foreign country. For instance, I remember once going to a large mosque, a citadel in Cairo, and going in there to pray, and it's just a fantastic experience and same with a Hindu temple. I've done the same in Singapore. It doesn't matter where you are around the world. In Latin America, I remember going to say some prayers on the top of a Mayan Temple or an Aztec Temple. I later found that this Temple was known for its local warrior god of which many people still pray toward today. So, these are just examples of sacred places that many people have called energy centers around the world that you may want to visit.

25. Higher Self Visitation Exercises

This idea revolves around cultivating a relationship with your higher self, and one of the exercises and rituals that I've seen is to commune with yourself in a visual way. You would do a visualization or an enhanced meditation where you see yourself meeting with your higher self in a sacred place to commune.

Communing with yourself is a doppelganger type of exercise, because you're meeting with your higher self. To begin this exercise requires your relaxed imagination. Some people may see themselves as a bird or a falcon flying through the sky, through the forest and landing at the sacred place. Then they morph back into their bodies or into a human being who then walks to the sacred door. Upon opening the door they walk into a great hall and see this other self of theirs up on a throne or maybe at the end of a table, and they sit down and talk to that other self. That other self can look like yourself or it can look like another race; it can have long dark hair, long blonde hair, it can have a crown, or it can be a man or a woman, it doesn't matter. It's what you feel your higher self or higher source would look like. It's part of your soul.

You ask that person questions, deep questions, questions you want to answer, maybe advice, and it may give you something deeper and more authentic than even your own wisdom. It may be able to give you calmer and more sincere answers to questions that you are seeking to answer. The answers may even be different or modified in some way than the ones that you've already come up with by yourself. So, it's a fantastic exercise. Or you could just go there to be thankful, and to be safe with this person, and to commune with this other side of yourself, this higher side that is tapped into the source of all energy.

26. Mantras

The next section is about prayers and mantras. Sometimes it can be a perfectly good prayer that you've either written by yourself or someone else has written, like the serenity prayer by Reinhold Niebuhr, which is quite famous, or the St. Joseph prayer or any other great prayer. People may use it as a mantra, or just a short prayer that you just may use one word, like God or prosperity or whatever, and you can say this again and again to yourself, silently in meditation or during the course of your day and that's an example of a prayer mantra that you may have.

27. Prayer for Others and Forgiveness

The next section is praying for others, which is extremely important, and that includes forgiveness. Many people pray for the welfare of their loved ones or family, their children, their relatives, and so forth, and then there's other types of prayers. You may want to pray for somebody who is a leader or pray for someone you dislike or pray for someone that you want to forgive, whether they're living or not living. People who have gone into group therapy or private therapy may at times send a letter to someone or leave a letter on someone's tomb or even facilitate a rite of penitence.

28. Hospitality Exercise

Another type of spiritual practice or ritual would be just hospitality and this goes back really to the ancient peoples of many cultures, whether it's an Eskimo culture or a German culture or a Russian culture. I'm just giving you some examples. When a stranger comes to your door and they're hungry, that type of hospitality, feeding the individual, the traveler, with food and drink and hospitality and maybe even a place to sleep, all of these things are important. I think maybe today hospitality has been transformed into helping making sure people have a safe place to stay and some healthy food to eat when they're in need. It's very, very important. In its highest form, hospitality honors those who are contributing to humanity and you give or tithe to others to support their good works.

29. Celtic Action

The next type of ritual would be more of a Celtic prayer ritual. Many Celtic prayers are based in action and activities. There are examples of people who say little prayers along with their actions. They may say a prayer when they do the harvest or a prayer when they serve dinner or a prayer when they kill a beast that will be used to feed the family or the tribe. I'm giving you some shamanic examples, but these are just examples of how specialized prayers are used for everyday activities and everyday events.

30. Sabbath

The next section is about the Sabbath, having a sacred day during the week, which is about the Sabbath. It could be on Sunday, but in other cultures it may be Friday or a Saturday or another day. Whenever it is, it's having quality time to either take care of yourself or take care of your family members or your children or to commune with nature or to be silent or even in some cultures to commune with your ancestors or those that have gone before you. These are all examples of how the Sabbath is important. Many people attend mass or a church service or a temple or other type of service. So all of this is part of keeping one day special where you can rest and recuperate and be prepared for the rest of your week.

31. Environmental Exercise

The next section is about an eco-ritual or environmental harmony that's based on many Shamanic cultures, but particularly some of the pagan cultures of ancient Europe and Asia and in Africa. It involves having environment respect and respect for animals, much like the Native Americans did, and respecting the trees and the plants and the crops and even like I had read a book by **** once and he even talked about it. He's a famous Buddhist and he even talked about how he ate his meals he would sometimes pray while eating or pray before or after eating, pray in thankfulness to all the animals and the trees that worked in harmony to create his food. So, all of us want to keep nature unpolluted and protect our forests and our rivers and our mountains, and environmental respect goes back and is a timeless part of spirituality and respect from the beginnings of time until now in many cultures. Trees and other things have been used, either before Christ or afterwards, in the use of sacraments or rituals.

32. Character Exercise

The next section is about precepts or character building and this is about a ritual. Whether you look at Marcus Aurelius or Ben Franklin, or at the present moment people like Steven Covey, you're looking at your daily activities and how you can be a better person each day and maybe you might make a list at the end of the day of the things you did well and the things you didn't do well and see if you can improve on them. In 12-step lingo, the 10th step focuses on being a good person each day and trying to be good to others and make amends to others when you can. Even if you read the writings of Pythagoras or Buddha you would see this same type of character building virtues in their practices, and with Socrates as well, in virtues and ethics in their daily lives.

33. Tithe Exercise

Giving and receiving is part of our world. Generosity and giving are timeless activities based on love and compassion. There are 2 types of giving. 1) giving to those who need help 2) giving to those who are expanding their talents, abilities, and craft. Either type of giving is inherently good. Practice giving your time or money to that which inspires you divinely.

Sacraments of Life

Most cultures and believers have been exposed to the initiatory rites and hidden sacraments of life, but here I will discuss each of these sacraments as a personal initiation.   The first sacrament is baptism, and that is when we are purified by water. But we all are purified by water on a daily basis, and we need to be reborn every day, and we have that birth and that baptism in life.   Every day that you wake up, you have an opportunity to do great things, and to be great to yourself and other people.

Number two is a confirmation or a commitment to the spiritual path, and every day you can daily substantiate your intentions.   You can make this confirmation daily to yourself that you will be your best and do the best.   It is sort of a right of passage.   It is like an awakening of sorts in life where you become old enough and you realize it is time to do your best and take care of yourself and stay in tune with the universe and be all you can.   The next initiation is Eucharist, and that is accepting the body and blood of the "Chosen One" by connecting yourself to God and to the universe, and you put the seven deadly sins behind you.   You transmute them and you connect to the life force by setting aside pride and lust and anger, greed, gluttony, envy and sloth.

The next rite of passage is atonement and penance.   Penance when you go through a catharsis of letting go, and you make a vow to yourself to atone and stay mentally and spiritually clear and awake, and that is again putting the mental garbage of ego and pride and discouragement aside, and clearing the path for you to be awakened in life, and aware and mindful on a daily basis, and be present in the now.   Through this penance, through this clarity, this state of mind, you become pure.   The next level is spiritual matrimony.   All persons may achieve a holy relationship and a love and a marriage when we engage a "God consciousness", and what is God consciousness?   It is a full-blown connection and awareness of the beneficence of the universe, and you are connected to it as a heir and child, as a creation of the universe, and you know you are part of the whole.   That is the matrimony, the marriage that some people claim in mystical experiences.   To become enlightened, one would achive ordination.   When an individual becomes illumined and transformed and reborn, he or she is ordained in the spirit, and that is really when an individual knows he or she has transcended into a higher order of living by going through all of these other steps of baptism and confirmation, and the Eucharist, penance and matrimony, and you become a spiritual master.   The last initiation is extreme unction, and this is important, because when you forgive and you let go and you allow your old self to die out, then this death becomes an awakening, and you become reborn in spirit and in life while alive in this consciousness.

I2K – Illumaniti C2K – Consciousness in the New Age –

13 Steps to Energizing Consciousness

1) **You must Cultivate a** cooperation of the self and ego with Spirit. If we as students of metaphysics realize that a harmonious relationship with our inner self and higher self is a relationship of peace and success, then our cooperation will allow a fusion with our Spiritual and material life. It is an inside job and the work is esoteric in nature, and we must clear ourselves on the inside to free our consciousness and fill ourselves and our souls with constructive Spirit energy.

2) **Two** is concerned with our external environment and our Spiritual and physical associations. If we associate with like minds of Spiritual nature, we can excel. Persons who encourage and support our growth are good for our expansion and health. Many authors throughout history have advocated researching those whom we admire to model ourselves after. Ask for those you admire for insight. Learn to be the best by associating with the best. Put yourself in the company of those who are constructive. Act as if you are your ideal. Become The PERSON you Want to BE. Learn to reinvent yourself and grow toward your desired character and image. Avoid those persons who are destructive. Engage life, stay active, help others, and they will help you.

3) Thoughts are things. We think, therefore, we are. We are beings of thoughts, energy, and creation. What you think is emitted and sent out from you. Your thoughts attract like thoughts. Through constructive thinking, focus, concentration, action, gratitude, thanksgiving, and praise, these things will be brought back to you. Be very specific in your petitions and desires and allow for the best results to manifest for you even if they are different from your desire. You are a magnet for higher good if you project good.

4) The courage to think what you want and to take action towards what you seek is an ultimate power of consciousness. This type of mental control and focus may allow you to see in your mind's eye what it is you want and will do. This type of advanced imagination, visualization and mental planning prepares you for each day's actions and work. In the present moment, we can do all we can toward our objectives. We cannot change yesterday or do tomorrow's work. We must use our mind and actions toward today's goals and mission.

5) This chapter is dealing with the effective use of our Spiritual and emotional energy. If we do not live in the present and dwell on what was wrong in our past, then our present energy is dissipated in favor of the ills of the past. Do not blame your past for anything. You are capable of all things new. Your body and mind can be renewed

altogether with continued Spiritual and metaphysical focus. Our emotions are very important. If we use our present days, present thoughts, and visualization toward our desired ideals and mix this with our constructive emotion; then, we can move quickly toward what we want from life.

Moreover, we can sometimes move effortlessly towards our True Place in conjunction with the will of our Higher Power. Additionally, prolonged grief and self-sabotage can destroy our growth and health. Moreover, resentments, anger, hatred, and self-loathing will indeed attract more of the same into your life. Severing from the past, asking for forgiveness, making amends, doing a self-appraisal and proper atonement if possible will free our minds from self-tyranny.

6) **L**ove is the quality of thought and emotion that will propel us into "peace of mind" and also great success. Love all there is. Focus on the good, the best, the constructive, and the beauty of life. See the best in all there is. See the good that results from the world. Meditate on the people that have been good to you, the creation all around you, the good that happens every day, the inventions for the good of humanity, and the positive happenings around the world that occur each and every day. Learn to love all and love yourself, and love will be attracted to you. Love is a form of gratitude, harmlessness, peace, kindness, and care. Thinking love and giving love will liberate you into the forth dimension of thought. Think of how you have been blessed, protected, and guided throughout your life. Yes, lessons have been learned, and further happiness, peace, and success may be yours if you stay on the path of Spiritual abundance.

7) Build an ideal vision of yourself as strong, healthy, and vigorous. You are bringing to yourself of invisible element that which is ever drawing to you more of health, strength, and vigor. With this being said, thoughts of great things: thoughts of health, thoughts of harmonious relationships, thoughts of peace, and thoughts of wealth will project into the world and mould your life. People will be attracted to you to add to and increase your world and journey. Health, beauty, confidence, and success are mostly a state of mind. We have all seen an average-looking superstar be regarded as absolutely beautiful. Thus, how we think and carry ourselves most definitely affects how we are perceived and how we feel day-to-day.

8) Freedom to believe in success and greatness is vital for mastery. Allowing ourselves to aggressively engage life while heading towards our purpose is fundamentally important. People who relegate themselves to something that they do not want to do for their lifetime are inhibiting their happiness and their potential service to humanity. As with the birds and other animals, each person must seek out our natural expression. Nobody is stopping us from following your dreams. We are not animals. We have consciouse choices and an abundance of opportunity in this world. Ask yourself what you want to be, who you want to be with, and how and where you want

to live. Think about the possibilities. Coalesce the choices of: jobs, careers, business ventures, and creative alternatives that you have available in your present and future. Imagine all of the great gifts and prospects that you have in your life because of our ability to imagine excellence and achievement.

9) "All things" are possible with cooperation with your consciousness and the fundamental laws of energy that animate the universe. The power of the universe works in and through you. We are all consciouse parts of the Infinite Power, a power ever carrying us up to higher, finer, happier grades of being. Good is on your side. Righteousness is your partner in life. If you join forces through cooperation and contemplation with your Higher Awareness, then you will believe that only good is possible and thus, faith will be induced through your harmonious and thankful mindset and actions. Your thought energy has the power to command the elements, and quiet the mental storm. Your Spiritual Consciousness as a part of the great whole has in it the germ of creative power. Never underestimate yourself, never speak with discouragement to others, do not continue doubting opportunity and your good. Nothing is impossible. If you can see its achievement in your mind, it may be possible. Impossible is a simple-minded response and excuse to doing anything. Rather ask: Why not?

10) There is a reality of the body and its capabilities. The body can grow, heal, renew, learn, and do great works. However, we must realize that rest, exercise, diet, fellowship, and peaceful activities are vitally important to this growth and renewal. The body or temple is renewing itself daily with new cells and cleansing itself of the old. The mind is integrating new information and processing old information every day and night. The mental computer must be maintained and charged and go through catharsis from time to time. When we permit our body and soul to grow, heal, and regenerate, we become more effective each day. The Universe is working with us at every moment to help produce what we need. We should focus on maintaining an effective state of mind which allows flow to be received. We must be ready to receive the gifts of the Universe in the highest form. We would be wise to allow the gift to be given and have an open mind and heart to the ideal that comes to us.

11) Are you ready for a better life? Do you believe that all things good are possible? Can your thinking and your character be transformed toward higher thought and toward constructive thinking of Spiritual abundance? If we were to approach things as if they are possible, then would we have a better chance of success and happiness? Become open to that inflowing force of Spirit and abundance. Allow yourself to change for the better, take action, and move forward toward your highest good.

12) Begin your day with taming your mind with Mindful and constructive thoughts. Feed your body, mind, and soul with the best food, information, and sacred energy. Act, think, and be good to yourself and others. Ask and petition from your higher power all that you want. Hope and pray for the best to happen to you and everyone.   Bless, praise, and be mentally thankful for all things good. Empower yourself and your Spirit with love, gratitude, kindness, harmonious thinking, harmless action, and serenity. Your highest gifts will be provided by the Universe as long as you do not resist the assistance of abundance and continue to be contemplative in action.

13) New thinking and ideas are possible. This can be called insights or prescience. It is a simple adjustment to the way we use our mind. Try to *not* complain for a one whole day. Try to stop blaming. Quit making excuses for not doing what you desire. Your thoughts and character can be reinvented. You can be reborn. New flows of thoughts and ideas will naturally come to you as you maintain a more unadulterated mindset. Your mind and thinking can transcend into a new constructive awareness. It takes time and effort, but anyone can do it. We must be persistent. In life or business we must press on in mind to achieve the successful results that we desire. Each day is a new opportunity to engage new ideas, new awareness, and engage several successful tasks. We can begin and start the nucleus of activity upon any idea.

Conclusion: We can perform tasks effectively and efficiently toward our ideals and goals. We must see in mind or imagination the thing we plan in its completed form, the system or method organized and in working order, the movement or undertaking advancing and ever growing stronger, constructive, and more profitable. To spend time and force in looking back and living in the past can be avoided.   We can avoid counterproductive people, places and things if needed.

There is no need to speak or think of the past. The past has taught us lessons. We may not have achieved what we wanted or been treated fairly. However, we have learned a lesson and need never to participate in a destructive engagement again. Risks we must take, but our new risks will be calculated because we will be prepared for anything that comes our way. We can avoid certain things and engage healthy ones. All experiences are valuable for the wisdom they bring or suggest. When you have once gained wisdom and knowledge from any experience, there is little profit in repeating it, especially if it has been unpleasant,

I2K – Illumaniti C2K – Consciousness in the New Age –

Our thought is the unseen magnet, ever attracting its correspondence in things seen and tangible. As we realize this more and more clearly, we shall become more careful to keep our minds set in the right direction on self-development. It is our divine right to have a rich and full life with abundance. The Universe may send people to help us and guide us. We can accept their help and create win-win relationships where all benefit.

You Spiritual and material life should both be important to you. What you make important to you will grow. If you make your family, your success, and your wealth important, all will grow in your life. When you blend your visionary mind, your emotion, your thoughts, and your action toward what you want, you will indeed meet your goals and dreams, particularly if you maintain a harmonious and grateful relationship with the timeless power of the Universe.

Continue to cultivate mindfulness, awareness, and your imagination. See in your mind's eye what you truly want. Do not be afraid to ask for anything that is good for you and for all. Hold that picture of completed success in your mind. Project it on the picture screen of your mind with sharp and defined clarity. Claim it as yours and thank the Universe for providing it to you. Be thankful, affirm your blessings, and take action toward what you want. Send it out of your mind into the world with thanks and confident expectation knowing that the thing you desire or something better will come into your life or unfold in your life's journey.

Make Your Resolution to Become Great

"Belief is the energy that animates the wings of the soul." -- GM

In this short little essay, we will discuss several top gurus in self-help, spirituality, success, and prosperity, and we will illuminate a few of their best ideas so we can remember how to manifest our DESTINY.

1. **LESSONS:** There are lessons in every mistake. If you read Dr. Napoleon Hill's or Oprah Winfrey's work, you will understand that there may be the seed of success in every failure. The great news with any failure or mistake is that you NEVER need to repeat it. You can move on to new heights.

2. **The Magic of WORDS:** Write your goals down. There is magic in writing them down. If you read the great ideas of top management consultants like Bryan Tracy, you'll see that there are scientific advantages in writing out your objectives. Write down your ideas and your chief goals. Write down places you want to see, things you want to do, skills you want to learn. If you do two or three things a day, then by the end of the year, you'll have over a thousand things done. It is amazing how the mind works to allow the subconscious mind to assist us even while we are sleeping or resting. When you put an idea in your mind, the deeper consciousness actually begins to work on the ideas and seek solutions around the clock.

3. **Purpose and What You DON'T WANT:** Great writers of history have often talked about cultivating a chief purpose or determining a labor of love. Generally, narrowing our focus and directing our energies can make us very powerful and boost our momentum, but there is a flip side. We all need to know what we want to do and go after our desires and ideas with all of our effort, but we also need to know what we DON'T want in life and the types of activities that we need to avoid or get rid of. There are the various types of actions or omissions that we need to avoid so that you can be successful. Some success gurus such as Stuart Wilde have claimed that "half of life's success" is avoiding crazy people or toxic situations. Moreover, the great Tony Robins has also taught that you need to know what you DON'T want, and

then TARGET what you DO WANT and go after it with extreme fervor and enthusiasm.

4. **Start Early and Be on Time:** Whether you're talking about Abraham Lincoln, Dr. Oz, or the "tortoise and the hare", it's always best just to get started and get moving, and sooner or later you'll cross that finish line with great success. Even Abe Lincoln said if you gave him a few hours to chop down a tree, he would spend most of his time sharpening the axe… If you just get started, you could take the tree out quicker, faster, and better without stress or haste. Some great lessons there, whether it's Abraham Lincoln or Dr. Oz, great lessons.

5. **Authenticity:** To stay true to yourself, be authentic and maintain a warrior like humility. One of the definitions of humility is remaining teachable. Thus, if you have your ears and your eyes open and stay aware, no matter how smart you are, no matter how many degrees you have behind your name, you will learn things, and you might gather information that is priceless. Even Clint Eastwood, in one of his famous Westerns, said, "A man's life in these parts often depends on a mere scrap of information." Whether you read Socrates, Buddha, or Shakespeare, Know Thyself and Maintain Humility and Awareness.

6. **HEALTH**: Put your mental, spiritual, and physical health first. Whether you're taking a class from a self help guru like the great Suze Orman or you're learning a lesson from another great teacher, you're putting your mental spiritual and physical health first, and that means you're investing in yourself. Taking care of yourself, developing self-love, developing self-regard, all of these characteristics are invaluable. If you treat yourself well, you'll invariably be able to treat other people well also. Keep showing up for the mental, physical and spiritual gymnasium to be your best.

7. **The ZONE:** Every year, many self-help books are released with a general theme and focus. One of the biggest themes in the last few years has been how to get out of your comfort zone—encouraging people to go and do something different, learn to do something new, take a new path. It is solid advice to have healthy routines, to do things well and right and not deviate from what works

for you. However, there's also something to be said for taking calculated risks and getting out of your comfort zone. People like the great T. Harv Eker, an excellent author and an excellent speaker, have talked at length about this. Pick up the phone and call somebody you want to meet or speak with. Call somebody and ask for help as a mentor; say, "Look, I know you've done this type of business before. You're great at it. Can you help me? Can you teach me what I need to know to maybe be good in this business, too?" Therefore, reaching out, trying something new, engaging in new activities makes you feel alive. This overall theme in many books is a very powerful message.

8. 8.   **Manage Your Mind:** The next idea is to "Mind your business and manage your mind." If you read great books or listen to great speeches by sales experts like Zig Ziglar, you'll understand that we all need to "prime our pumps" to get our mind moving. We should focus on building our mind power every day. A lot of the great self-help authors talk about buying self-help tapes or reading books, having "learning CDs" in your car, or downloading audiobooks. In today's world, managing your mind has a much greater meaning: We need to keep our mind clear and running smoothly, like getting the oil changed in a vehicle, having a computer run a virus check, or deleting junk out of the cache or the temporary files of a computer so it can operate more quickly and be more responsive. That's what we're talking about when we say managing your mind. It's one thing to mind your own business—that means to focus on what you need to do for yourself and not what other people need to do. It's another thing to talk about the effective and efficient management of your own mind.

9. **PEACE OF MIND:** The next principle is to become a conscious observer of your mind and your ego. Famous writers on the subject of consciousness such as Eckhart Tolle or Thich Nhat Hanh talk a lot about learning to meditate or to quiet the mind, allowing you to observe your thoughts and sharpen your mental activity. But the next level beyond these teachings is learning to discern the difference between your spiritual consciousness and your ego consciousness. This is the ability to know what is good, constructive, and beneficial for YOU—to determine which are harmonious actions and which thoughts are just destructive and selfish, aren't going to get you anywhere, and waste your time and mental energy. Mental energy is precious, and if you get bogged down in just one resentment or one angry thought, you can lose half of your day or

your whole day. Some people are capable of spending weeks or years being angry and upset, and they've basically wasted their time and their lives when they could have been a more productive member of society or spent more time with their children or family.

10. **ROUTINES:** The next thought is about healthy routines and why you should have them. It doesn't matter who you are or what age you are, whether you're 14 or 92. We all need to eat right, sleep right, and have healthy fellowship with other human beings so we can continue to cultivate friendships and relationships and be able to express ourselves with others. You also need to get the type of exercise that you need. Now, exercise can be broken down into several areas. There's physical exercise, there's mental exercise, and then there's the spiritual gymnasium. It's important to have a nice blend of all of these things. If you pick up a book on anxiety or depression—even ADHD, bipolar disorder, addiction, or any type of debilitating situation that an individual may have—there's going to be a couple of sections in the book about letting go of destructive habits and picking up constructive and beneficial habits. Not addictions, but constructive and beneficial activities. Activities that make you feel alive, that give you joy and benefit your life and those you love. That's the key to this step is maintaining healthy routines. There is a retired admiral who made millions of dollars by giving speeches who wrote a book describing getting up and making your bed in the morning. I believe the message is that we can learn to "Do one thing right when you wake up and the rest of the day will continue to follow that expression of good will." Therefore, healthy routines of fellowship/social interaction, REM-quality sleep, exercise, and diet/nutrition are all very important. The acronym for Fellowship, REM, Exercise, and Diet would be FRED. The scientific value of FRED is that all of these elements stimulate proper well-being and production of serotonin and dopamine; they create a healthier body on a physical level.

11. **RESPONSIBILITY:** The next step is really about how to practice effective and rapid response—how we can learn to do things well. I've known top surgeons in my life, and some can do an operation in 30 minutes and others might take three or four hours. Both surgeons are safe and not being negligent, not going too fast. An on-schedule and quick surgery reduces risk of infection

and complications. As for surgeons, some people are more comfortable doing things really well at a certain speed, and I think it takes practice, practice, practice to achieve new levels of skill. Recently, I heard a speech by Mike Singletary, the famous linebacker, and he said he practiced eye–mind awareness skills and rapid response using techniques that I had read that were used by "secret spiritual factions" hundreds of years ago. Singletary said he would stand up and take his two fingers and hold them out on each side and try to spread his awareness and depth perception by being able to see things in the corners of his vision to try to understand movements better. The great linebacker used these exercises to be able to see, or READ, the other team's offensive line much better than any other linebacker in our lifetime most probably.

This is about practicing rapid response—not reaction, but conscious responsiveness. If you watched Tom Cruise in his famous movie, "The Last Samurai," his character was subject to the same interplay: Cruise's character was told to use "no mind," to keep practicing and keep developing his skills. By the end of a season, he was able to respond with his sword lightning fast, with utmost skill. I believe that the great time management consultant Tim Ferris talks a good bit about being able to do things really well, and he uses an example of trying to respond to as many emails effectively as you can within a certain amount of time and getting that part of your day behind you. As a lawyer, I say be careful with emails and hasty responses, but for non-legal communications, it sounds like a great exercise.

12 . **You Are What You SEEK:** The next step is to regulate what you take in, both physically and mentally, on a conscious level. If you read books by the great Dr. Deepak Chopra or many other great spiritual and self-help writers, they talk about the types of negative information that you choose to take in and whether that is healthy for you. The types of people, places, and things that you encounter, or allow yourself to encounter, are also important to determine whether these interactions are healthy for you. But then, really, the next level beyond that is the concept of "you are what you eat." In this day and age, in the new science of the 21st century, if you're not feeling well or you're not feeling right, you need to find out what types of foods and what types of liquids and water quality you consume. Mental fitness is one issue, but physical and dietary

issues can affect the mind. We must make sure that our bodies are at the optimum level.

Today, the talk out of Silicon Valley and pro sports is about brain hacking and peak performance. I have not read Tom Brady's new book, but I can presume many of these issues address this topic directly. All of these young performers are taking various vitamins and minerals and nutrition, eating certain things and taking certain proteins and herbs. Some of the vitamins are even synthetic forms of vitamins that may maximize mental and physical condition. We're not talking about steroids, and we're NOT talking about SPEED either. Whether it's Ritalin, Adderall, or steroids, this topic is NOT about the use of doctor-prescribed drugs.

In sum, there's a whole new Generation X out there, and they're monitoring and maximizing their mental, physical, and spiritual health through the use of testing, computers, diet, herbs, proteins, minerals, and vitamins, along with exercise, hiring coaches, and everything else. It could be called a buckshot approach that people are using, where they are trying to turbo-charge themselves physically, mentally, and emotionally. So, be discerning about what you eat and what you consume so you can maximize yourself each day, whether it be during the day or at night while you sleep. There are even things to do to improve your sleep, as well. Sleep is important because a good, quality REM sleep is what allows your mind to function at its best the following day. Some people have specific foods, meditations, exercise, or supplements they do before sleep to make sure they have a great sleep pattern.

13 **BE YOU AND BE ALIVE:** The next step is really to find out what makes you feel alive. Make a list out. Write down things that you enjoy doing, or maybe you don't enjoy doing, or write down things you MAY enjoy doing. Go try them out if you can, or find somebody who is good at a particular activity you want to try out and talk to them. Say, "Hey, I know that you ski at the mountain every year. Would you take me with you and teach me?" There's lots of great hobbies in life. It's not just getting out of your comfort zone; this is really about learning new skills and being alive. Unless you experience or try certain things, sometimes it's difficult to know what really makes you feel good. Sometimes people fall into a certain type of job or labor of love when they didn't even know they enjoyed it, they just happened to experience it or go try

it out. A lot of authors have talked about this. Sometimes you have to just go work at the donut shop to find out whether or not you enjoy dealing with pastries and customers every day. What makes you feel alive? What makes you feel wonderful? What gives you energy? What animates you in life? If you read great authors like Martha Beck or T. Harv Ekar, they talk a lot about this. Even Dr. Chopra talks about the word "Dharma" and your purpose in life and what animates you. In sum, this is about getting into your groove and finding where you can best operate, maximize your potential and serve humanity.

14 **Your Environment:** The next step is, who do you associate with? The famous Kim Blanchard and other authors talk about how attitudes rub off on us. Basically, they've analyzed various types of people, whether it's in the United States or other places, and the income, happiness, and success rate of the average person is about equal to the people they associate with, generally speaking. So, if you can, associate with people who are smarter than you, faster than you, better than you, people maybe you can learn something from. Maybe it will rub off. Maybe it will allow you to strive to beat those goals and to do better and better and better. Surround yourself with people who can help you grow. Remember, there is something called "vibration." If you put two tuning forks next to each other and ring one of the forks, the other fork will begin to vibrate at the same level.

15 **What Is Your Energy Type:** The last principle is to know your matrix. Really, this idea is about understanding and knowing thyself. Whether you go back to Shakespeare, or to Buddha, or to Jesus Christ, or any of the great philosophers, teachers, and masters of time or history, they're going to say to know yourself, particularly if you want peace of mind. Know who you are. Know your authentic self and connect with that authentic self. If you read Ralph Waldo Emerson or Thoreau, don't be a "cow in the herd" just following the rest of the herd. You can be unique, march to the beat of your own drum, and be the best you can be. Maybe you can do something unique, different, and wonderful. Be who you're supposed to be. Remember, the unique cornerstone is always necessary at the end of the day to make the architecture of the traditional blocks form a complete building. Thus, "Beat to your own Drum, Stand Tall, and BE PROUD.

How to Get What You Want – Prof Wattles and George Mentz, Esq. - Summary

1. Mind has been described as the substance by which the soul is given the chance to experience existence in the physical world.

2. There is no greater service to humanity than to make the best of yourself.

3. YOU must get rid of the last vestige of the old idea that there is a Deity whose will it is that you should be poor, or whose purposes may be served by keeping you in poverty.

4. In order to know more, do more, and be more we must have more; we must have things to use, for we learn, and do, and become, only by using things. We must get rich, so that we can live more.

5. To get rich, you need only to use your will power upon yourself.

6. Do not talk about poverty; do not investigate it, or concern yourself with it. Never mind what its causes are; you have nothing to do with them.

7. What concerns you is the cure. Use your will power to keep your mind OFF the subject of poverty, and to keep it fixed with faith and purpose ON the vision of what you want.

8. If your heart is set on domestic happiness, remember that love flourishes best where there is refinement, a high level of thought, and freedom from corrupting influences; and these are to be found only where riches are attained by the exercise of creative thought, without strife or rivalry.

9. Getting what you want is in the effective application of a cause

10. The cause of success is always in the person who succeeds

11. The key to success is finding the cause of success and replicating the cause.

12. Use your strongest faculty, and you can cultivate any faculty

13. Can I have to realize you are potential and empower you must use your faculties in your skills effectively

14. You must learn to create conscious action.

15. Cultivate Gratitude and Harmonious Mind

16. Poise is the combination of peace and power that can be applied to each action or thought.

17. Act in a Certain Way in all you do with effectiveness, efficiency and providing value or increase to all.

18. Power consciousness is the secret to success. Power consciousness is what you feel when you know that you can do a thing and you KNOW exactly how to do it.

19. Belief is the other key to mastery because you MUST believe that it is possible for you to achieve success, while you must believe that you can learn how to do something effectively and flawlessly.

20. The more steady and continuous your faith and purpose, the more rapidly you will get rich, because you will make only POSITIVE impressions upon Substance; and you will not neutralize or offset them by negative impressions.

21. The picture of your desires, held with faith and purpose, is taken up by the Formless, and permeates it to great distances-throughout the universe

22. You must bring things from your conscious mind into your subconscious so that you will know instinctively how to do tasks. Truly knowing in your deeper mind is similar to when you drive a car and speak on the phone as your deeper mind is Knowingly and unconsciously guiding your driving.

23. We must learn how to effectively send ideas, techniques, and plans from the idea phase in mind into our subconscious mind. We can use tools such as auto suggestion and making a picture board, or use incantations to imprint ideas onto our sub consciousness

24. Learn to utilize your existing assets in the now

25. Learn to affect the function of each task you engage

26. Do all you can in the nail feel your present place in the now

27. Make use of your present environment

28. Form of a clear conception of which you see in your mind and on the picture screen of your mind

29. You can phone clear conceptions of each task that needs to be achieved

30. Become more successful by using constructively the business you have now

31. We may secure more friends buy using constructively the network you already have

32. We may achieve greater domestic happiness by the constructive use of the love that already exists in your home.

33. You can get what you want in the future by concentrating all your energies upon the constructive use of whatever you are in relation with today and the NOW

34. A surplus of life causes evolution, growth, and opportunity.

35. Take an interest in all people you meet me the business of socially and since their leaders of the best for them. This will create the advancement for you

36. Respect yourself the absolutely charged to all put life into every act and fought and fixed power consciousness fought up on the fact that you are entitled two big promotion it will come as soon as you can more than feel your present place in everyday

37. Our you must be well rounded and balanced and body and mind and soul and in love.

38. Focus on doing what must be done. Take action in areas that can be effective in your life.

39. Whenever you find yourself hurrying, call a halt; fix your attention on the mental image of the thing you want, and begin to give thanks that you are getting it. The exercise of GRATITUDE will never fail to strengthen your faith and renew your purpose.

40. Man may come into full harmony with the Formless Substance by entertaining a lively and sincere gratitude for the blessings it bestows upon him. Gratitude unifies the mind of man with the intelligence of Substance, so that man's thoughts are received by the Formless.

41. Man must form a clear and definite mental image of the things he wishes to have, to do, or to become; and he must hold this mental image in his thoughts, while being deeply grateful to the Supreme that all his desires are granted to him. The man who wishes to get rich must spend his leisure hours in contemplating his Vision, and in earnest thanksgiving that the reality is being given to him.

42. Too much stress cannot be laid on the importance of frequent contemplation of the mental image, coupled with unwavering faith and devout gratitude. This is the process by which the impression is given to the Formless, and the creative forces set in motion.

43. The whole matter turns on receiving, once you have clearly formed your vision. When you have formed it, it is well to make an oral statement, addressing the Supreme in reverent prayer; and from that moment you must, in mind, receive what you ask for.

44. In order to receive his own when it shall come to him, man must be active And he must do, every day, all that can be done that day, taking care to do each act in a successful manner and he must so hold the Advancing Thought that the impression of increase will be communicated to all with whom he comes in contact.

- *There is a thinking substance from which all things are made, and which, in its original state, permeates, penetrates, and fills the interspaces of the universe.*

- *A thought, sent into this substance, Produces the thing that is imaged by the thought.*

- *Man can form things in his thought, and, by impressing his thought upon formless substance, can cause the thing he thinks about to be created.*

- *In order to do this, man must pass from the competitive to the creative mind; he must form a clear mental picture of the things he wants, and hold this picture in his thoughts with the fixed PURPOSE to get what he wants, and the unwavering FAITH that he does get what he wants, closing his mind to all that may tend to shake his purpose, dim his vision, or quench his faith.*

- *That he may receive what he wants when it comes, man must act NOW upon the people and things in his present environment.*

- *In order to do this, man must pass from the competitive to the creative mind; he must form a clear mental picture of the things he wants, and do, with faith and purpose, all that can be done each day, doing each separate thing in an efficient manner.*

- Man may come into full harmony with the Formless Substance by entertaining a lively and sincere gratitude for the blessings it bestows upon him. Gratitude unifies the mind of man with the intelligence of Substance, so that man's thoughts are received by the Formless.

- Man must form a clear and definite mental image of the things he wishes to have, to do, or to become; and he must hold this mental image in his thoughts, while being deeply grateful to the Supreme that all his desires are granted to him. The man who wishes to get rich must spend his leisure hours in contemplating his Vision, and in earnest thanksgiving that the reality is being given to him.

- In order to receive his own when it shall come to him, man must be active; and this activity can only consist in more than filling his present place. He must keep in mind the Purpose to get rich through the realization of his mental image. And he must do, every day, all that can be done that day, taking care to do each act in a successful manner. He must give to every man a use value in excess of the cash value he receives, so that each transaction makes for more life; and he must so hold the Advancing Thought that the impression of increase will be communicated to all with whom he comes in contact.

I2K – Illumaniti C2K – Consciousness in the New Age –

The Garden – A Story of Planting Seeds and Growth

1. **G is for Good and God** – Know that if you enter the garden and begin your work, that the universe and life force will allow you to farm your good and reap what you sow
2. **A is for Attention and Atonement** – If you are willing to clear away the debris in your garden, till it, weed it, and make it a place that is conducive to growth, then your mental garden will be ready for seeds.
3. **R is for Ready to Receive** – Clear the garden, and ready the mind to receive new and good seeds, plants and crops.
4. **D is for Decide** – You must select the seeds, the best for the climate and season. You must commit to planting and putting them into the right place to receive sunshine, light, nutrients, and rain.
5. **E is for Emotionalize and Efforts** – You must put your feelings behind your work and your seeds/ideas. These ideas have been planted, and now it is time to back the ideas up with action, boldness, joyful effort, and enthusiasm.
6. **N is for NOW** – You clear the weeds in the now, you plant the seeds in the now and you nourish the garden in the now, you protect the garden in the now, you let go of the process and allow the seeds to grow in the now, and we harvest in the now. We have a plan in the now, and we execute. We have the prospects willing to be satisfied and we deliver. The recipient happily rewards our joyful efforts.

Prayers for Protection, Love, Forgiveness and Health

Protection Prayer – Recite 3X
Father's Love, Forever Bright
Divine Mothers' Emerging Light
Surround My Soul With your Affection
Your Super Power Gives Me/Us Protection

Love Prayer – Recite 3X
Mighty Peace is in My Heart
Where Love Prevails, a Magic Art
I Close My Eyes, I am Made Whole
As God's True Love Engulfs My Soul
In My Mind & Three Times Three
I Feel All Love AND Unity.

Forgiveness Prayer – Recite 3X
Purity is My Divine Right
The Force of Calm is in My Sight
The Power of Healing Light Within
Free Forever of Any Sin
I Clear Away All Old Debris
Where Now I Master Destiny.

Health 3X Prayer
My Every Cell in Harmony
My Body Whole Perfect & Free
As Love Lives Strong With ALL Above
My Heart Transcends to Master Love
Where Body and Soul Are Healed & Whole
The Supreme Force Renews My Soul.

I2K – Illumaniti C2K – Consciousness in the New Age –

Acronyms to Inspire your Subconscious Mind

1. **IC** – Instead of "I think, therefore I Am", Goddard or a Physicist may say, "I see, therefore, it is"
2. **BU** – You must be yourself, and become who you were meant to be.
3. **UR** – You must know that your is-ness is your connection to the universe.
4. **CU** – You must see yourself as you want to BECOME or HAVE.
5. **IB** – I become what I think about all day.
6. **NU** – The power is within when you are aware of your connection.
7. **YU** – Why NOT you. Your divine inheritance is waiting for you to accept the gift.
8. **6 ¢** - Sixth Sense - Use your inspiration and creative intuition to follow your dreams and manifest your destiny.
9. **B4U** – You must be "FOR YOU", and mentally a proponent for your self development, self regard and improvement of your life. Be on your own team. Be your own cheerleader. Don't be a mental house divided.
10. **BC** – You will eventually Be what you see on the picture screen of your mind. Creative visualization is very powerful.
11. **URNRG** – You are energy. You are pure being. Be aware of your spiritual energetic creative self. Be aware of the signs and symbols of the universe's desire to assist you. You can tap into the unlimited supply of the universe with your awareness of the **NOW**.
12. **CN2BU** – Seek inside of yourself. It is an inside job. Look deep within to clear away the past, build yourself up, learn all you can, and take action to be your best so that you may help yourself, your loved ones and humanity.

Quotes on Prosperity and Abundance

- "Wealth is not his that has it, but his who enjoys it." —Benjamin Franklin

- "Life is a field of unlimited possibilities." —Deepak Chopra

- "He who is plenteously provided for from within, needs but little from without." —Johann Wolfgang von Goethe

- "Take full account of the excellencies which you possess, and in gratitude remember how you would hanker after them, if you had them not." —Marcus Aurelius

- "Whenever anything negative happens to you, there is a deep lesson concealed within it, although you may not see it at the time." —Eckhart Tolle

- "If you want to change who you are, begin by changing the size of your dream. Even if you are broke, it does not cost you anything to dream of being rich. Many poor people are poor because they have given up on dreaming." — Robert Kiyosaki

- "Ideas are the beginning points of all fortunes." —Napoleon Hill

- "When you are grateful fear disappears and abundance appears." —Anthony Robbins

  "Everything in the universe has a purpose. Indeed, the invisible intelligence that flows through everything in a purposeful fashion is also flowing through you." —Dr. Wayne Dyer

- "Gratitude is an attitude that hooks us up to our source of supply. And the more grateful you are, the closer you become to your maker, to the architect of the universe, to the spiritual core of your being. It's a phenomenal lesson." — Bob Proctor

- "Living in Abundance and Success is a Reasonable Option" —Magus Incognito

- "You have a divine right to abundance, and if you are anything less than a millionaire, you haven't had your fair share." —Stuart Wilde

- "Prosperity is not just having things. It is the consciousness that attracts the things. Prosperity is a way of living and thinking, and not just having money or things. Poverty is a way of living and thinking, and not just a lack of money or things." —Eric Butterworth

- "Most folks are about as happy as they make up their minds to be." — Abraham Lincoln

- *"And he shall be like a tree planted by the rivers of water, that bringeth forth his fruit in his season; his leaf also shall not wither; and whatsoever he doeth shall prosper."* —Psalm 1:3

- "The Constitution only gives people the right to pursue happiness. You have to catch it yourself." —Benjamin Franklin

- "Not what we have But what we enjoy, constitutes our abundance." — Epicurus

- "Gratitude is the vital ingredient in the recipe for Faith" —Magus Incognito

- "We may divide thinkers into those who think for themselves and those who think through others. The latter are the rule and the former the exception. The first are original thinkers in a double sense, and egotists in the noblest meaning of the word." —Arthur Schopenhauer

- "The key to every man is his thought. Sturdy and defiant though he look he has a helm which he obeys, which is the idea after which all his facts are classified. He can only be reformed by showing him a new idea which commands his own." —Ralph Waldo Emerson

- "All truly wise thoughts have been thought already thousands of times; but to make them really ours we must think them over again honestly till they take root in our personal expression." — Johann Wolfgang von Goethe.

- "Great men are they who see that spirituality is stronger than any material force; that thoughts rule the world." —Ralph Waldo Emerson.

- "All that we are is a result of what we have thought." —Buddha

- "Wealth is the slave of a wise man. The master of a fool." —Seneca

- "Happiness is not in the mere possession of money; it lies in the joy of achievement, in the thrill of creative effort." —Franklin D Roosevelt

- "Money is like manure. You have to spread it around or it smells." — J. Paul Getty

- "Liberty is not a means to a higher political end. It is the highest political end." — Lord John Dalberg-Acton

- "We are what we repeatedly do. Excellence, then, is not an act but a habit." — Aristotle

- "Money is like love; it kills slowly and painfully the one who withholds it, and enlivens the other who turns it on his fellow man." — Kahlil Gibran

- "Empty pockets never held anyone back. Only empty heads and empty hearts can do that." —Norman Vincent Peale

- "The thief cometh not, but for to steal, and to kill, and to destroy: I am come that they might have life, and that they might have it more abundantly." — John 10:10, KJV

- "Prosperity is not without many fears and distastes, and adversity is not without comforts and hopes." —Francis Bacon

- "It is health that is real wealth and not pieces of gold and silver." — Mahatma Gandhi

- "Desire is the starting point of all achievement, not a hope, not a wish, but a keen pulsating desire, which transcends everything. When your desires are strong enough you will appear to possess superhuman powers to achieve."— Napoleon Hill

- "Move out of your comfort zone. You can only grow if you are willing to feel awkward and uncomfortable when you try something new." — Brian Tracy

- "You can open your mind to prosperity when you realize the true definition of the word: You are prosperous to the degree you are experiencing peace, health and plenty in your world." —Catherine Ponder, *Open Your Mind to Prosperity*

- "There is a science of getting rich and it is an exact science, like algebra or arithmetic. There are certain laws which govern the process of acquiring riches and once these laws are learned and obeyed by anyone, that person will get rich with mathematical certainty." —*Wallace D. Wattles*

- "Within you right now is the power to do things you never dreamed possible. This power becomes available to you just as soon as you can change your beliefs." —*Dr. Maxwell Maltz*

I2K – Illumaniti C2K – Consciousness in the New Age –

Other Books By Dr. Mentz

List on Amazon

- Quantum Bliss
- 50 Laws of Power
- Spiritual Wealth Management
- It Works
- Magic - The Power of Positive Mindfulness
- Wealth Management
- 25 Greatest Business Books
- The Law of Attraction & Prosperity Bible
- The Illuminati Handbook
- The Illuminati Code The Secret Powers of the Mind - Man's Search for Extraordinary Success and Meaning
- Masters of the Secrets
- The Vikings - Philosophy and History – From Ragnar LodBrok to Norse Mythology
- Prayers and Principles of The World's Religions Wisdom Proverbs Maxims

About the Author

George Mentz JD MBA, CWM - Global Keynote Speaker - is a celebrated speaker, IBA award winning author, professor, international lawyer and founder of the first USA Certification Training Body to be ISO 29990 Certified or Accredited for Quality and Training. He is a recognized wealth management authority and the first lawyer in the United States to be triple credentialed in international law, management, investment advisor law, and financial planning. Mentz holds a Doctor of Jurisprudence (JD) an MBA degree in international business, and an international law certificate qualification along with relevant government law licenses. Mentz's renowned teachings, fiscal policy ideas, and wealth technology have been used in the top banks, government employees, national campaigns, Fortune 500 companies, and financial institutions around the globe. Mentz is former Wall Street Investment Banker, award winning professor, and the CEO of the Global Academy.

Mentz has been seen on television and press as a pioneer in financial psychology, success, and wealth education. He is the author of over 30 books and manuals, and many bestsellers. While in graduate school, Mentz was the Chairman of the Tax and Estate Planning Law Review and he is also a two-time national award winning professor . In recent years, Mentz was a Brain Trust Member in Financial Media, to the Dream Team of Advisor FYI (part of National Underwriter), and Mentz has even been an accepted legal expert in FINRA/NASD Securities Arbitration. A frequent analyst quoted in press, television, and radio, Mentz is also a popular endorser and public presenter. Mentz has been a keynote speaker in the USA, China, Arabia, Asia, Caribbean, & Latin America for Major Wealth Management Conferences, National Associations, Wall Street Firms, and with webcasts to hundreds of thousands of people. Mentz is the founder of the GAFM Global Academy of Finance and Management ® in 1995 which has over 50,000 members in over 150 countries.

---

[i] The Science of Being Great" by Wattles – Elizabeth Towne Publishing 1914

- Excerpts, paragraphs, and selected content in this book are from pre-1925 writings of: Wallace Wattles, Christian Larson, William Walker Atkinson, and Genevieve Behrend

Other References or Authors of Interest

Allen, J. (1998). *As You Think*. Ed. with introduction by M. Allen. Novato, CA: New World Library

Behrend, G. (1927) Your Invisible Power. Montana: Kessinger Publishing.

Carnegie, D. (1994). *How to Win Friends and Influence People*. New York: Pocket Books. http://www.dalecarnegie.com

Carlson, R. (2001). *Don't Sweat the Small Stuff About Money*. Location: Hyperion. Previously published as *Don't Worry Make Money* http://www.dontsweat.com.
Chopra, D. (1996). *The Seven Spiritual Laws of Success*. London: Bantam Press. http://www.chopra.com

Collier, R. (1970). *Be Rich*. Oak Harbor, WA: Robert Collier Publishing. http://robertcollierpublications.com

Covey, S. R. (1989). *The 7 Habits of Highly Effective People*. London: Simon & Schuster. http://www.stephencovey.com

Dyer, W. (1993). *Real Magic: Creating Miracles in Everyday Life*. New York: HarperCollins. http://www.drwaynedyer.com

Gawain, Shakti (1979). *Creative Visualization*. Mill Valley: Publisher. http://www.shaktigawain.com

Haanel, Mentz (2006). *How to Master Abundance and Prosperity - The* Master Key System *Decoded*. Location: Xlibris Pub.

Carlson Haanel Wattles, Mentz (2005). *The Science of Growing Rich*. Location: Xlibris Publishing.

Hill, N. (1960). *Think and Grow Rich*, New York: Fawcett Crest.

His Holiness the Dalai Lama & Howard C. Cutler (1999). *The Art of Happiness: A handbook for Living*. London: Hodder & Stroughton. http://www.dalailama.com

James, William (1902). *The Varieties of Religious Experience*. Location: Publisher.

Maltz, Maxwell, MD. Psycho-Cybernetics. New York. Pocket Books 1960

Marden, O. S. (1997). *Pushing to the Front, or Success under Difficulties*, Vols 1 & 2. Santa Fe, CA: Sun Books.

Mentz, G. S. (2006) *Other Books and Summaries on The Secrets of Life and Abundance:* http://gmentz.com

Mulford, Prentice (1908). *Thoughts are Things - Essays Selected From The White Cross Library*. Location: Publisher.

Murphy, J. (1963). *The Power of Your Subconscious Mind*, New Jersey: Prentice Hall.

Ponder, C. (1962) *The Dynamic Laws of Prosperity*, Camarillo, CA: DeVorss & Co.

Roman & Packer (1988). *Creating Money*: Tiburon, CA: Kramer. http://www.orindaben.com

Price, J. R. (1987). *The Abundance Book*. Carlsbad, CA: Hay House. http://www.johnrandolphprice.com

Smiles, S. (2002). *Self-Help: With Illustrations of Character, Conduct, and Perseverance. Oxford, UK: Oxford University Press.*

Tracy, B. (1993). *Maximum Achievement: Strategies and Skills That Will Unlock Your Hidden Powers to Succeed.* New York: Fireside. http://www.briantracy.com

Troward, Judge Thomas (1904). *The Edinburgh Lectures on Mental Science.* Location: Publisher.

Wattles, W.D. (1976). *Financial Success through the Power of Thought [The Science of Getting Rich].* Rochester, Vermont: Destiny Books. (Written originally around 1910).

Wilkinson, Bruce (2000). *The Prayer of Jabez.* City, OR: Multnamah Publishers. http://www.prayerofjabez.com

Bibliography

Other References or Authors of Interest

Allen, J. (1998). *As You Think.* Edited with an introduction by M. Allen. Novato, CA: New World Library.

Aurelius, M. (1964) *Meditations*, trans. M. Staniforth, London: Penguin. The Bhagavad-Gita (1973) trans. J. Mascaró, London: Penguin World's Classics..

Behrend, G. (1927) *Your Invisible Power.* Montana: Kessinger Publishing.

Carnegie, D. (1994). *How to Win Friends and Influence People.* New York: Pocket Books.

Carlson, R. (2001). *Don't Sweat the Small Stuff About Money.* New York, USA: Hyperion.

Chopra, D. (1996). *The Seven Spiritual Laws of Success.* London: Bantam Press.

Collier, R. (1970). *Be Rich.* Oak Harbor, Washington: Robert Collier Publishing.

Coelho, P. (1999) *The Alchemist*, trans. Alan R Clarke, London: HarperCollins.

Covey, S. R. (1989). *The 7 Habits of Highly Effective People.* London: Simon & Schuster.

Dyer, W. (1993). *Real Magic: Creating Miracles in Everyday Life.* New

York: HarperCollins.

Eker, T. H. (2005). *Secrets of the Millionaire Mind: Mastering the Inner Game of Wealth.* New York: HarperCollins Publishers.

Emerson, R.W. (1993) *Self-Reliance,* Dover Publications.

Gawain, Shakti (1979). *Creative Visualization.* New World Library, Mill Valley USA.

Bishop Bernard Jordan (2007). The Laws of Thinking: 20 Secrets to Using the Divine Power of Your Mind to Manifest Prosperity." (2007) *(9781401917968): Published by Hay House and Bishop E. Bernard Jordan: Books*

Hill, N. (1960). *Think and Grow Rich.* New York: Fawcett Crest.

His Holiness the Dalai Lama, with H. C. Cutler (1999). *The Art of Happiness: A Handbook for Living.* London: Hodder & Stroughton.

James, W. (1902). *The Varieties of Religious Experience.* Longman Publishing, London, UK.

Jeffers, S. (1991) Feel the Fear and Do It Anyway, London: Arrow Books.

Lao-Tzu's Tao Te Ching (2000) trans. T. Freke, introduction by M. Palmer, London: Piatkus.

Maltz, M.. (1960). *Psycho-Cybernetics.* New York. Pocket Books.

Marden, O. S. (1997). *Pushing to the Front, or Success under Difficulties,* Vols. 1–2. Santa Fe, California: Sun Books.

Mentz, C. W. H. (2007). *Masters of the Secrets: And the Science of Getting Rich and Master Key System Expanded: Bestseller Version.* Bloomington, Indiana, United States: Xlibris Corp.

Mentz, C. W. H. (2006). *How to Master Abundance and Prosperity—The Master Key System Decoded.* Bloomington Indiana: Xlibris Pub.

Mentz, C. W. H. (2005). *The Science of Growing Rich.* Bloomington, Indiana: Xlibris Publishing.

Mentz, George S - *Other Books by Mentz.* http://www.lulu.com/gmentz

Mulford, P. (1908). *Thoughts Are Things: Essays Selected from the White Cross Library.* G. Bell and Sons, Ltd., LONDON, 1908.

Murphy, J. (1963). *The Power of Your Subconscious Mind.* New Jersey: Prentice Hall.

Peale, N.V. (1996) *The Power of Positive Thinking,* New York: Ballantine

Books.

Ponder, C. (1962). *The Dynamic Laws of Prosperity.* Camarillo, California: DeVorss & Co.

Price, J. R. (1987). *The Abundance Book.* Carlsbad, California: Hay House.

Roman, S., Packer, D. R. (2008). Creating Money: *Attracting Abundance.* Tiburon, California: H. J. Kramer, Inc., published in a joint venture with New World Library.

Scovell Shinn, F. (1998) *The Game of Life and How to Play It*, Saffron Walden: C.W. Daniel.

Seicho-no Iye (生長の家). Books by Dr. Masaharu Taniguchi.

Smiles, S. (2002). *Self-Help: With Illustrations of Character, Conduct, and Perseverance.* Oxford: Oxford University Press.

Thoreau, H.D. (1986) *Walden and Civil Disobedience*, introduction by M. Meyer, New York: Penguin.

Tracy, B. (1993). *Maximum Achievement: Strategies and Skills That Will Unlock Your Hidden Powers to Succeed.* New York: Fireside.

Troward, T. (1904). *The Edinburgh Lectures on Mental Science.* DODD, MEAD & COMPANY: New York.

Wattles, W. D. (1976). *Financial Success through the Power of Thought: The Science of Getting Rich.* Rochester, Vermont: Destiny Books.

Wilkinson, B. (2000). *The Prayer of Jabez.* Colorado Springs, CO USA, OR: Multnamah Publishers.

Manufactured by
Amazon.ca
Bolton, ON